COMMUNICATING
•••••• F O R ••••••
TEAM BUILDING

COMMUNICATING
• • • • • • • FOR • • • • • •
TEAM BUILDING

Baden
EUNSON

JOHN WILEY & SONS
BRISBANE • NEW YORK • CHICHESTER • TORONTO • SINGAPORE • WEINHEIM

First published 1994 by
JACARANDA WILEY LTD
33 Park Road, Milton, Qld 4064

Offices also in Sydney and Melbourne

Typeset in 11.5/14 pt Garamond

National Library of Australia
Cataloguing-in-Publication data

Eunson, Baden.
    Communicating for team building.

    Bibliography.
    Includes index.
    ISBN 0 471 33560 6.

    1. Communication in management. 2. Communication
    in organisations. I. Title.

658.4

Edited by Bookmark Co. Pty Ltd
All illustrations by Mike Spoor

Printed in Singapore

10 9 8 7 6 5 4 3

PREFACE
· · · · · · · · ·

Teamwork and team-building are very fashionable concepts at the moment. And that is only fitting and desirable: the team way of doing things can be extremely effective and satisfying. In order to prevent team-work and team-building becoming unfashionable, however, it's necessary not only to know what teams do well, but also to know what they do not do well. *Communicating for Team Building* can help you to understand both sides of the question.

In this book you will learn about the rise of the team organisation, the pros and cons of teams, and the nature of the underlying principles of group dynamics, leadership and power. You will also discover the practical communication skills of non-verbal sensitivity, listening to others and giving feedback to others, using group problem-solving techniques, running effective meetings, resolving conflict, and presenting the team's ideas to the outside world.

Throughout the book, you will find numerous exercises to help you build your skills. More information about the specific points in the text is contained in numbered endnotes at the back of the book. If you wish to read still further in this area, a large and up-to-date reference list is provided.

Baden Eunson

CONTENTS

• • • • • • • • • •

1

TEAMS

WHY TEAMS?

As we prepare to step into the twenty-first century, people are beginning to organise themselves in new ways, both inside and outside the workplace. Groups or teams are coming to be seen by many as being more effective than either individuals operating by themselves or the departments, committees and production lines of traditional organisations.

As we shall see, this in fact is not always the case — teams, in whatever shape or form they appear, are sometimes extremely effective, and sometimes disastrously ineffective. The key to knowing when to use teams, and to realising their potential for excellence, lies in knowing all about their strengths and weaknesses.

If we want to understand such strengths and weaknesses, then we need to understand the communication processes that take place within groups or teams. *Communicating for Team Building* may prove to be a powerful tool in helping you to understand and master such processes.

Examples of these communication processes are shown in figure 1.1 (overleaf). They include:
- listening and questioning skills
- the skills of giving feedback to others
- the skills of giving and seeking feedback about oneself
- the ability to seek out and process information
- the ability to use and choose between group methods such as consensus, brainstorming and nominal group methods
- effective meeting skills
- the ability to understand and influence role-playing and norm-formation in groups
- the ability to understand and influence leadership and empowerment behaviour
- the ability to understand and influence conformity and cohesiveness in groups
- sensitivity to non-verbal behaviour
- the skills of representing the team to others.

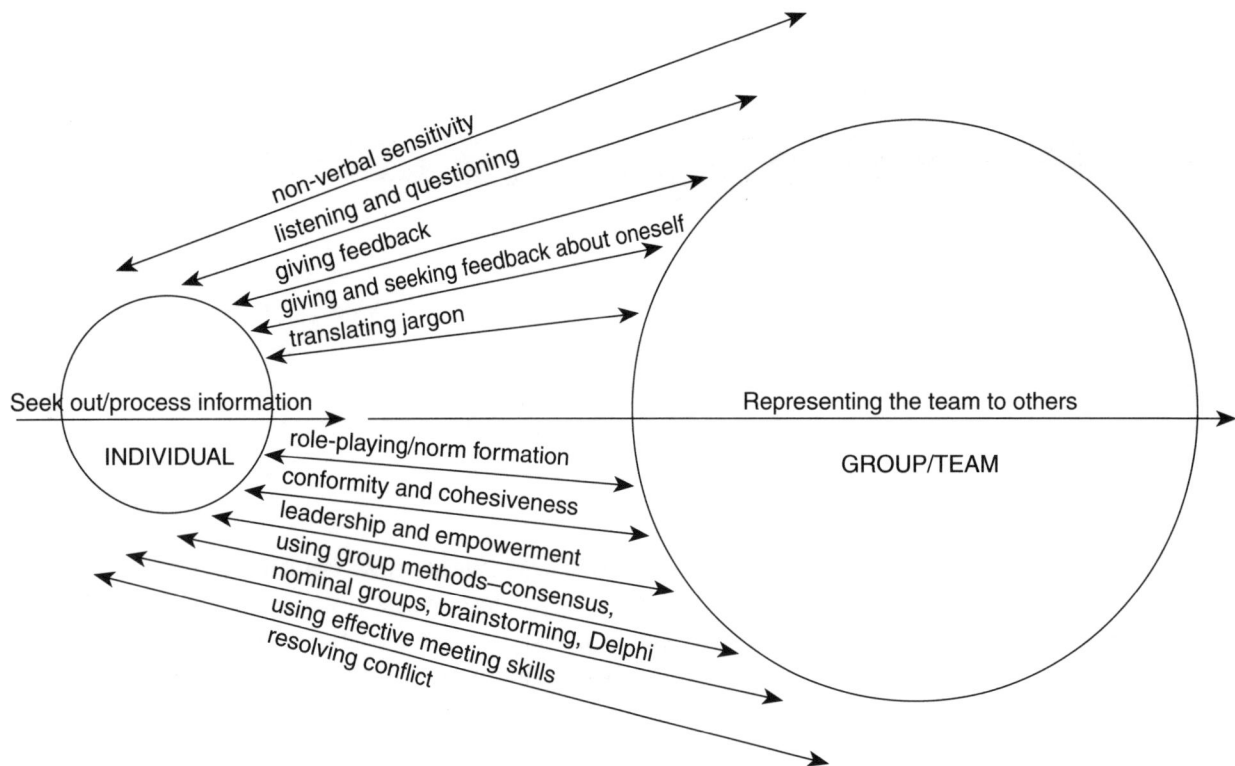

Figure 1.1: A model of communication in teams

To gain some insight into these processes, take some time now to complete the following questionnaire.

EXERCISE

A:
YOUR TEAM'S
PERFORMANCE

Think of a team or group of people with which you spend a fair amount of time. Ideally, it should be a group with which you have worked, or are currently working. It might be a full-time job or a part-time job; it might be a paid job or a volunteer activity. If these experiences aren't available to you, think of other types of work, such as schoolwork, or think of a hobby or friendship group or sporting team.

Answer all the questions as best you can, marking the Strongly Agree–Strongly Disagree columns for each question. When you have completed the questionnaire, record your scores according to the instructions that follow it.

Note
Strongly agree = SA
Agree = A
Neutral = N
Disagree = D
Strongly disagree = SD

In this team . . .	SA	A	N	D	SD
1. I can express any opinion I like.					
2. People's words are consistent with their body language. What they say is not contradicted by their gestures, postures or eye contact.					
3. We know each other's strengths and weaknesses, and we work to complement each other.					
4. Nobody listens to me.					
5. People interrupt each other.					
6. People will always give objective feedback. Total honesty is the only way to operate, and no-one takes criticism personally.					
7. People trust each other so much that I would be willing to discuss my failures, knowing that this information wouldn't be used against me later.					
8. People tend to play destructive roles rather than constructive ones.					
9. If we had secret ballots to decide issues, the decisions reached would be vastly different to those we currently reach.					
10. People with big egos and big mouths make it difficult for others to get a word in edgeways.					
11. I get embarrassed when I get a compliment, and tend to dismiss it.					
12. We are loyal. For example, I defend our performance when outside the team.					
13. Our meetings tend to be ad hoc, crisis events.					
14. We share. If I have a success outside, I always acknowledge the team.					
15. It's okay to deliver bad news. We concentrate on solutions, not witch-hunts.					

(continued)

In this team . . .	SA	A	N	D	SD
16. I have so much respect for these people that if I had my own business, I would hire them using my own money.					
17. The saying 'It's hard to fly like an eagle when you're surrounded by turkeys' is true.					
18. We trust each other so much that any of us could speak outside the team on our behalf.					
19. The presence of high-status people stops others from expressing themselves freely.					
20. People focus upon causes, not symptoms.					
21. People would rather find a scapegoat than a solution.					
22. When we eventually reach a decision, we all feel as though we own it — we have a stake in seeing it successfully carried out.					
23. People would rather talk *about* others than *to* others.					
24. I get the silent treatment.					
25. If you want to know what's happening around here, try the grapevine, not our meetings.					
26. We always know how we are going; we have total feedback on our performance from outside the team.					
27. There are always winners and losers: the winners gloat, while the losers stew and plot revenge.					
28. My true allegiances lie outside the team.					
29. My goals are the same as the team's.					
30. You learn pretty quickly that it's better to work on something yourself and get the glory than to offer it to the team, only to see it hacked beyond recognition.					
31. Our goals are the same as the organisation's.					
32. We're too cocky — we all think we're so great that we make mistakes.					

In this team . . .	SA	A	N	D	SD
33. I can't do my job properly unless other members in the team do theirs.					
34. Reports and paperwork are done well.					
35. People would rather jump to a conclusion than climb to a solution.					
36. There are no superstars — we all check our egos at the door, and pull together.					
37. We keep our emotions tightly under control.					
38. We have a good idea of what we'll be working on a year from now.					
39. There always seem to be undercurrents of meaning, game-playing and hidden agendas — nothing is what it seems.					
40. Our leader is on a power trip.					
41. I'd be crazy to trust any of these people.					
42. We know that if we perform well, we will be recognised and financially rewarded accordingly.					
43. People misunderstand each other's written and spoken words.					
44. Our leader is too weak.					
45. Our meetings are extremely effective.					
46. I really don't want to be here. I just want a quiet life, a meal ticket and a comfy niche in the organisation outside this team.					
47. I would be willing to lose one-twentieth of my pay to retain a team member about to be laid off.					
48. I play a specialised role, but I've been doing it for too long — I feel typecast. I'm capable of other things.					
49. We have been given the power to achieve what we are meant to achieve.					
50. We could all achieve a lot more if we were working individually.					

How to score

1. Use the following system of scoring

SA	A	N	D	SD
5	4	3	2	1

for the questions whose numbers appear in the grid immediately below.

No.	Score	No.	Score	No.	Score	No.	Score	No.	Score
1		2		3		6		7	
12		14		15		16		18	
20		22		26		29		31	
33		34		36		38		42	
45		47		49					

2. Use the following system of scoring

SA	A	N	D	SD
1	2	3	4	5

for the questions whose numbers appear in the grid immediately below.

No.	Score	No.	Score	No.	Score	No.	Score	No.	Score
4		5		8		9		10	
11		13		17		19		21	
23		24		25		27		28	
30		32		35		37		39	
40		41		43		44			
46		48		50					

3. Once you have completed scoring, transfer the scores to the columns of the table below.

Motivation/ goals		Communication/ feedback		Status/ power		Team effectiveness		Decision making/ problem solving	
No.	Score	No.	Score	No.	Score	No.	Score	No.	Score
29		1		19		3		20	
31		2		40		7		21	
38		4		44		8		22	
42		5		49		14		35	
		6				15			
		9				16			
		10				17			
		11				27			
		12				28			
		13				30			
		18				32			
		23				33			
		24				36			
		25				41			
		26				46			
		34				47			
		37				48			
		39				50			
		43							
		45							
Total		Total		Total		Total		Total	
÷ 4		÷ 20		÷ 4		÷ 18		÷ 4	
Average		Average		Average		Average		Average	

Finally, transfer the values for all fifty questions to the graph on the facing page (figure 1.2). This will give you a rough but useful visual guide to how effective or ineffective your group or team really is. The higher your average score for each of the five areas recorded (page 7), then — at least in theory — the better your team's performance will be. The higher your line on the graph, the better things should be. The specific aspects of communication and other processes within groups and teams touched upon by these questions will be raised in the coming pages.

You might find it useful to have other members of your group or team complete this exercise. It might be wise if such an exercise was done anonymously. For example, ensure that everyone completes graphs in the same colour and type of pen, and then place graphs face downwards in a pile and shuffle them before pinning or taping them up for display. It might be interesting to complete this group exercise twice: once now, and once after the group has moved through *Communicating for Team Building* and is more familiar with the vocabulary and concepts of group dynamics, team building and communication skills.

Much of the effectiveness of group or team communication depends upon the constructive, or non-destructive expression of emotions; it is, therefore, always desirable to have a skilled facilitator run a session where a group or team completes an exercise such as this.

Remember, the 'data' revealed by such an exercise is fairly crude, and should be seen only as a beginning, not an end. It is by no means exhaustive. Even groups or teams with fairly low cohesiveness and effectiveness should be able to come up with at least ten other items or questions that could well be used in such an exercise. Nevertheless, the exercise can be a useful tool, but remember that it should be a tool for promoting group self-knowledge and development rather than recriminations and witch-hunts. The name of the game is team-building, not team-destruction.

Now that we have a general idea of what team effectiveness is, let's turn our attention to discovering why it is that teams and teamwork have become so important in recent times.

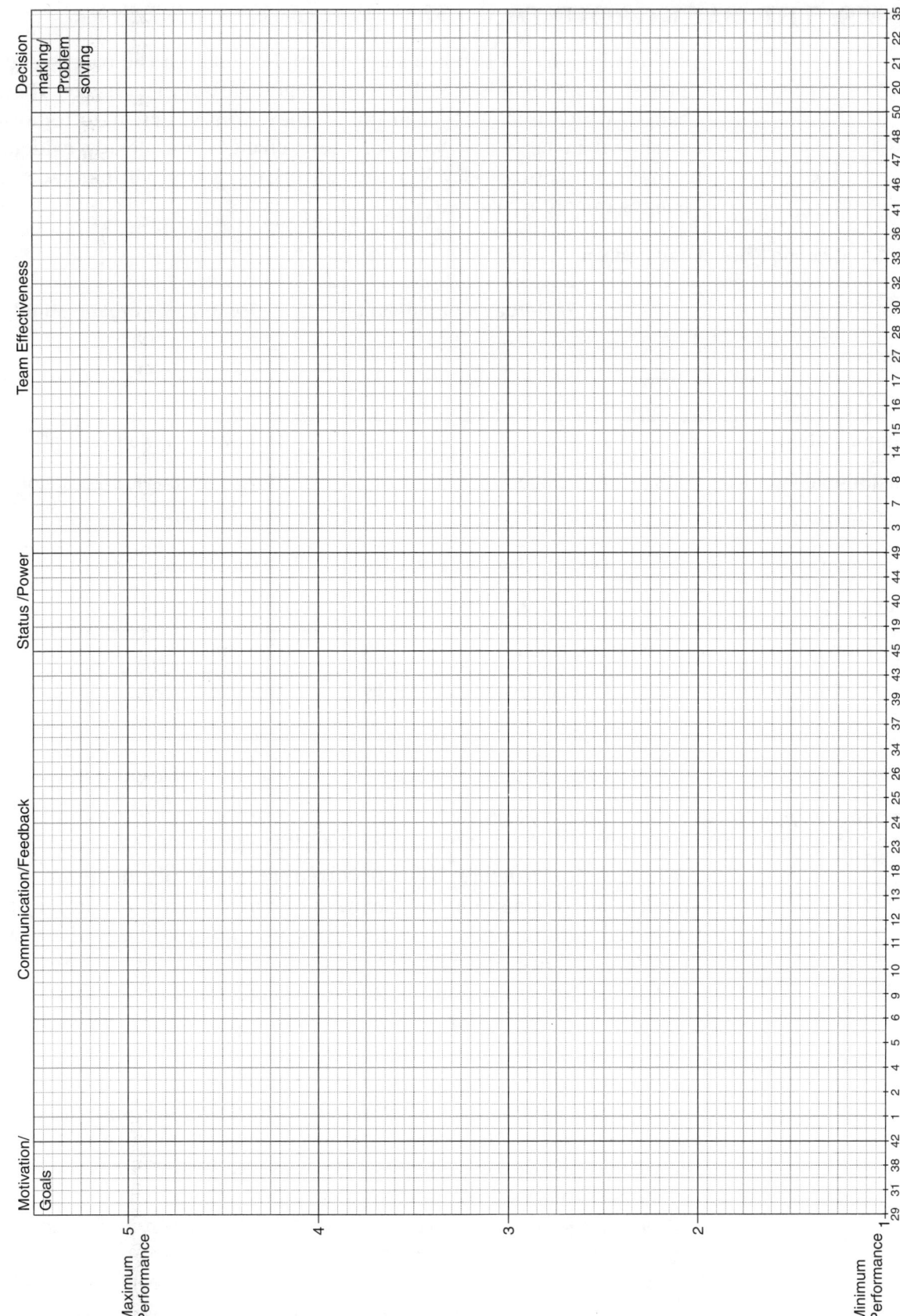

Figure 1.2: Team effectiveness graph

TEAMS: THE BACKGROUND

Organisations have been in a state of rapid change for the past twenty or thirty years, and teams have been an integral part of that change. The key changes which might occur in the journey from yesterday to tomorrow are shown in table 1.1. Some of these changes are already evident in many organisations today. Whether all organisations will embrace such changes, only time will tell.

Table 1.1: Differing types of organisation[1]

	Yesterday's organisation	Tomorrow's organisation?
Structure	Tall	Flat
Span of control	Narrow	Wide
Communication	Downward	Downward, upward, lateral
Decision-making	Autocratic	More democratic, participatory
Work relationships	Competitive	Collaborative
Work structuring	Departments, assembly lines	Groups/teams
Skill base	Specialisation/division	Multi-skilling
Innovation process	Sequential	Simultaneous
Power base	Official position in hierarchy	Expertise, skills
Differential status	High	Low
Control	External, upon individuals	Internal, within groups
Compensatory/pay focus	Seniority/individual	Merit/group

Changes in structure have occurred in many organisations. If we visualise an organisation as having a pyramid shape or profile, then traditional organisations tended to look like *tall pyramids*: there were many layers of decision-making from the top to the bottom.

This also usually meant that the average number of subordinates reporting to a supervisor or manager was small — there was a *narrow span of control*. The model was that of a military organisation.[2]

One-way communication, with messages flowing from the top to the bottom, was normal, as was *autocratic decision-making*, with power being the preserve of an elite at the top of the pyramid. It was often presumed that people lower down in the pyramid had neither the skill nor the interest to participate in decision-making.

Work relationships among departments and between individuals were usually *competitive relationships*.

Work was organised functionally, according to work units such as *departments and assembly lines*, which usually involved large numbers of people. Few people knew all other people in their work unit — in fact, many people worked alone, for all practical purposes.

Skills were organised according to principles of *specialisation and division of labour*; individuals and departments often did not understand the skills and tasks of other individuals and departments.

Change occurred via *sequential innovation*: research and development specialists thought up ideas for new commodities, which were then given to other areas, such as manufacturing, to implement. Product cycles were long — that is, products became obsolete only very slowly — and the input of others, such as customers, those doing the manufacturing, and marketing specialists, was rarely sought by the innovators.

Authority was largely based upon one's *official position in the hierarchy*; as with compensation or pay, this was often gained on the basis of seniority, rather than merit. Also, *high differential status* was obvious: individuals at the top of the pyramid had high status, with all that that meant in terms of respect from others, better working environments, better dress codes, etc., while the people at the bottom with lower status had none or few of these trappings.

Discipline was fairly firm, and based upon *external control of individuals*: it was presumed that individuals needed to be closely supervised if they were to perform at all. Rewards (and punishments) were allocated according to principles of *individual- and seniority-based compensation and pay*.

Changing world — changing organisations

This type of organisation worked reasonably well for years — indeed, centuries — but from about the 1960s onwards it was perceived that the traditional organisation was failing. This was due to a number of factors, as summarised in table 1.2 (overleaf).

As a result, many — but not all — organisations began to change. Multiple layers of organisation were seen to be strangling communication and responsiveness. The very function of numerous middle layers — the translation and reporting of information from the production centre at the bottom to the decision centre at the top, and the relaying of decisions in the other direction — was called into question as decision-makers at the apex of the pyramid began to believe — sometimes correctly, sometimes erroneously — that they could now access all such information directly via computers. The profile of organisations began to resemble *flatter pyramids* as layers were stripped out. For the first time in history, large numbers of middle-class middle managers began to lose their jobs as the idea of 'downsizing' took on (aided and abetted by pressures from economic recession and market competition).

As a result, those supervisors and managers who remained had to now deal with more subordinates — they had to cope with a *wider span of control*.

As organisations became more technology-dependent, more complex and more dependent upon quick reactions to changing markets, and as the limitations of large-scale or mass production became obvious, it made more sense for more and more groups or teams of specialists to work together.

Table 1.2: Change factors in modern organisations

Change factor	Explanation
1. Human motivation	Social science and management research seemed to suggest that many, if not all, people in organisations wanted to participate in decision-making — that in fact they were performing well below their maximum level because the system did not motivate them, and if they were given the opportunity to deploy their skills and intelligence, then total productivity would rise substantially.
2. Education	Younger generations of better-educated people were entering the workforce; these tended to be more assertive and less respectful of authority for its own sake than previous generations.
3. Future shock	The rate of social change seemed to be speeding up — automation, computerisation, globalisation, product innovation — and the bureaucratic rigidities of traditional organisations seemed ill-equipped to cope with these. Organisations seemed to be in a state of 'future shock'.
4. Information explosion	Jobs in many organisations became more and more complex. This reflected the 'information explosion' in many fields. Thus it became more and more difficult for individuals to know everything about a job or process. Individual generalists began to be replaced by groups of specialists.
5. Japanese challenge	The economies of the West began to wilt under the assault of Japanese manufacturing. Part of the secret of the success of the Japanese seemed to be production and decision-making that was broadly-based, and that was participative rather than autocratic.
6. Revenge of the customer	Linked to No. 5 was the point that the quality of many commodities — services as well as goods — was perceived to be lower than necessary, and increasingly assertive customers and clients were not going to accept this state of affairs any longer. Indeed, some customers were no longer content to be mere passive recipients of commodities: they wanted to have input into the very processes of production of those commodities.

This meant a radical change in workplace culture. You don't hoard information: you maximise its flow. You don't just stick to the one official channel: you open up new ones. Thus information flow was sped up by *upward, lateral and downward communication*.

You don't give orders to professionals: you persuade and negotiate with them. Thus *more democratic and participatory decision-making* became more often the norm.

It made little sense any more — if it ever did — for rival empires within the organisation, and even rival individuals within work units, to be competitive. The real competition was outside, not inside. Thus *collaborative relationships* became a necessity.

Large-scale departments and assembly lines were often broken down into smaller, more manageable *groups or teams*.

Change began to occur via processes of *simultaneous innovation*.[3] Design people began to work with manufacturing people, and marketing people — even customers — to design and refine products in a more dynamic way. This was partly a response to the shortening of product innovation cycles — that is, products were becoming obsolete more rapidly.

Also, it was perceived by many that team members would need to change the basis of skills deployment from specialisation to that of *multiskilling*, i.e., people would need to learn the skills involved in other jobs, not simply their own; the change would need to occur if for no other reason than members would need to understand the role of other members in the total output of the team: work functions would no longer be divided, but united.

This meant that supervisors and managers would need to derive their authority not so much from their official status as from their *expertise and skills*, and they would need to become less directive in trying to impose control.

Differential status — the gap between the highest of the high and the lowest of the low — was great in the traditional organisation. In a new, more democratic culture, this was no longer on, and thus *low differential status* became more desirable.

Control within organisations would shift from external control wielded over individuals to internal control, exercised within *self-controlling groups*.

Compensation and pay would become more *merit- and group-based*.

Customers or clients, rather than being an afterthought, floating somewhere below the bottom of the pyramid, would become the primary focus of the organisation. In fact, wherever possible, customers would become 'plugged into' the organisation by those inside the organisation listening to customers' needs and encouraging them to give input at design and production stages of commodities. The pyramid would be turned on its head.

This is a radical transformation we are talking about. The organisation would have gone from being a tall pyramid (figure 1.3(a)–overleaf) to being a flat pyramid (figure 1.3(b)) to being an inverted flat pyramid (figure 1.3(c)).

Will all organisations be like this? Not necessarily. Many organisations in the future will share the characteristics of the traditional organisation. Not all of these organisations will be unsuccessful, and not all of the people in them will be miserable. Indeed, there are no guarantees that the trends we have been witnessing might not be reversed.

Nevertheless, for many of the changes we have looked at, we do not have to wait until tomorrow — they are here today. The central feature of such changes is the group or team concept. Communication is the key to survival of the group or team — communication among members, and communication with the rest of the organisation and with customers.

In the following section, we briefly examine some of the strengths and weaknesses of teams. We then go on to look at teams in the broader context of group dynamics and group processes of communication.

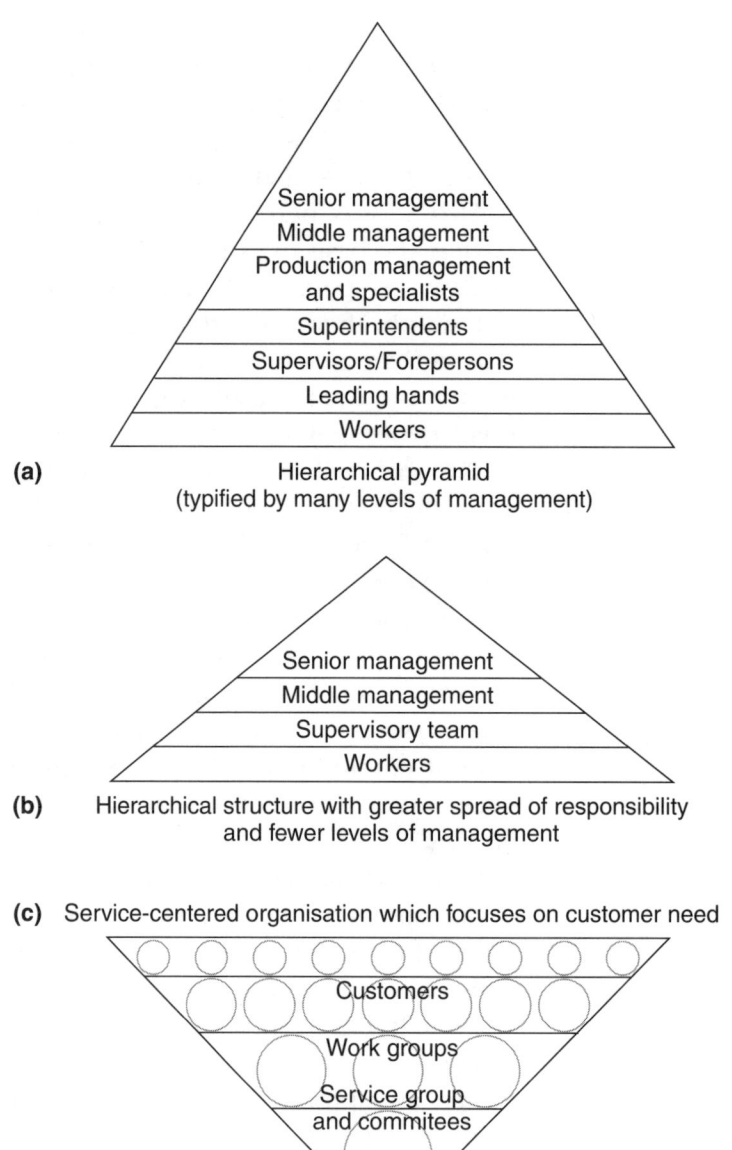

Figure 1.3: The changing shape of organisations

(Source: McPhee and McNicol, 1992. Reproduced with permission of the authors.)

TEAMS: THE GOOD NEWS AND THE BAD NEWS

Although teams and teamwork have played an increasingly important role in the structure of organisations in recent years, there are both positive and negative sides to working in teams. Table 1.3 (page 16) summarises the pros and cons of the concept.

On the positive side, teams have often been associated with substantial improvements in *productivity* when compared to traditional ways of structuring work. The US company General Electric found, for example, that productivity was increased by 250 per cent when it introduced team-based work (together with flexible automation and computerised systems) into its North Carolina lighting panel board plan. Johnsonville

Foods in Wisconsin introduced team-based production in 1976 and productivity has since risen by at least 50 per cent.[4]

The Melbourne plant of Trico, an automobile components manufacturer, switched to team organisation in 1984, and now performs well above other Trico plants in low wage areas such as Texas and Mexico, in fact, earning more than triple the return on investment typical in the rest of the components industry.[5]

Team- or group-based decision-making can be about *workplace democracy*, and thus has an ethical dimension to it as well. Some perceived that there was a contradiction between the democracy and freedom that people enjoyed outside the traditional workplace and the authoritarianism they encountered within that workplace. Teams or groups seem to bring democracy inside the workplace walls.

Mass production is a strategy that may no longer be sustainable by high-wage economies. The alternative may be to move to a flexible system or *batch production*, wherein smaller runs of more customised products — specialised steels, chemicals, drugs, synthetics, ceramics, computer hardware and software, even insurance policies, books and data bases — can be created. These require custom designing and ongoing servicing, and thus the distinction between goods and services blurs. Teams appear to be better suited to this production mode.[6]

There are more opportunities for skilled or *knowledge workers* in this technology-intensive world, and fewer opportunities for unskilled workers. It appears to be the case that the more educated and skilled workers become, the more self-motivated and self-directed they can be. In other words, there is less functional and behavioural need to have someone else tell them what to do, and thus the need for traditional leadership, supervision or management seems to be less pressing.

Teams can provide the ability to give a *rapid response* to changing circumstances: technology used in the production of goods and services is usually expensive, and thus it may be too expensive for workers to need to wait for managers to decide how to handle crises and rapidly changing circumstances.[7] It makes sense in these circumstances to delegate some decision-making to workers in groups or teams.

Teams can *reduce middle management costs*: large numbers of middle managers can either be dismissed or else put back in teams on a lower salary.

Speed is also of the essence when *more rapid product innovation* is needed. Teams are often cross-functional — that is, members come from differing departments or areas. Traditional relationships between such departments or areas are often characterised by bureaucratic red tape and territorial conflict, which, to say the least, slows down innovation. Teams can break down walls and get things done.

Finally, members of teams are often *multi-skilled* — that is, each member is not just a specialist, but knows some or all of the specialised aspects of other members' jobs. This often enhances communication among members, and it also means that if a member is away due to illness or for some other reason, then other members can fill in — the whole show doesn't collapse.

Table 1.3: Pros and cons of teams

Teams: pro	Teams: con
• can improve productivity	• productivity gains not guaranteed
• ethically desirable — bring democracy to workplace	• problems with accountability — hierarchy unavoidable?
• are better suited to batch production	• overload — management by stress
• are more suited to needs of knowledge workers	• a sign of 'corporate anorexia'?
• are able to respond rapidly	• change often cosmetic, semantic, 'ideological hype' — status quo preserved
• reduce middle-management costs	• not everyone is a team player
• foster more rapid product innovation	• multi-skilling not always effective
• multi-skilling enhances effectiveness and communication	

There may also be bad news about teams. Critics of both radical and conservative persuasions have had some rather unkind things to say about the concept.

On the negative side, *productivity gains cannot be guaranteed*. Productivity is often lost in setting up a new venture such as teams, and ongoing productivity is often not all that sensational.[8]

Teams also present problems with *accountability*. If a department or assembly line or group or team has a manager or supervisor, it is clear who is ultimately responsible and accountable for success or failure of that unit. If the manager or supervisor is non-existent, or plays a much-diminished decision-making role, then accountability becomes blurred. If the team gets it wrong, does the entire team get disciplined or fired? If the team goes really well, does the entire team get a bonus? Most people would probably be more comfortable saying 'yes' to the second question than to the first. Managers and hierarchy may thus be indispensable.[9]

The team concept, as applied in the US auto industry, has been criticised by some unionists as being a *'management-by-stress'* system, that is, it has produced more stress for workers by asking them to assume supervisory responsibilities (without necessarily giving more authority or pay), by removing necessary slack from the system with 'just-in-time' inventory systems, and by increasing harmful peer pressure in teams by introducing group bonus plans.[10]

Following from the previous two points, teams may not be so much a sign of organisational wellness as a sign of organisational pathology. It has become a byword — almost a cliché — that organisations these days need to 'downsize', to get 'lean and mean', and that usually means flattening the pyramid and removing entire layers of management, to cut costs and organisational 'fat' and to eliminate perceived barriers to communication. This usually means a massacre of the middle managers. If the cutting goes beyond fat into muscle, however, then, to mix metaphors, a state of '*corporate anorexia*'[11] will prevail, wherein a reduced group of frightened, embittered, disempowered middle managers will not be able to cope with the greatly increased decision load and span of control — share it as they might with team members. In these circumstances, 'downsizing' is just a cheap — but ultimately quite expensive — stunt to cut costs, dressed up in trendy rhetoric of 'team management'.

Also, sometimes the 'team revolution' introduced in some workplaces is merely a case of 'the more it changes, the more it stays the same' — in other words, 'teams' are merely *cosmetic or semantic changes*, or part of management 'ideological hype', and the status quo of departments and assembly lines still prevails.[12]

Not everyone is a team player. It is not uncommon for supervisors or team members to criticise, or even remove, other members who do not fit into the team model. Apart from the fact that teams are not always the ideal solution to all problems and situations, this is not the best way to deal with some individuals (who may be remarkably creative and productive rather than simply wilfully deviant).[13]

Finally, *multi-skilling may not always be effective.* Radical critics of teams argue that multi-skilling, a critical feature of many teams, often means de-skilling: jobs are simplified so that workers might be interchangeable (and often paid less), and also jacks of all trades may be masters of none. High technology requires that workers be specialists, and organisations should respect those specialisations, pay for them, and concentrate training on where it is needed, namely, communication between specialists.[14]

GROUP OR TEAM?

Are 'group' and 'team' the same thing? Not necessarily. A team is probably — and the matter is still open for debate — a special case of a group.

A team may be a collection of people who must work interdependently to achieve a common goal or output; if any one member of the collection can achieve his or her goal while another member cannot, then — by this definition — that collection would be a group rather than a team.[15]

Team members may differ from group members in that they may experience more open and honest communication, they may have a greater climate of trust, they may accept conflict as normal rather than abnormal, and they may feel more of a sense of ownership for their jobs and unit because they are committed to goals they helped establish.[16]

We can very easily get stuck in wordplay here. 'Teams' and 'team building' have a very emotional, positive ring to them. Yet the 'empowered teams' and 'self-managing teams' of the 1990s are not all that different from the 'semi-autonomous work groups' pioneered in Scandinavia in the sociotechnical job design experiments of the 1960s and 1970s.[17]

When people think of teams in the workplace, they often think of teams on the sports field, yet while that metaphor is often a misleading one (see 'Teams: The Sports Metaphor' following), this doesn't prevent people from using colourful sporting words and concepts. As Marilyn Collier remarks:

> *The word 'team' seems to conjure up warm and fuzzy feelings and images for people, and, therefore, they find it difficult not to use that term. The word 'group' seems to sound and feel cool, and has a more aloof connotation as used in the day to day language.*[18]

'Team building' is another distractingly exciting term. Strictly speaking, you can build a house, but how do you build a collection of human beings? 'Group development' might be a more accurate term for a process of unifying a collection of people so that they pursue goals with effectiveness, but it certainly sounds less exciting.

What people may mean when they use the term 'team' is simply 'effective group'. If they wish to use exciting terms like 'teams' and 'team building', and that excitement helps to motivate people to greater levels of effectiveness, then that's okay. Let's pour a small amount of water on that excitement by examining the sports metaphor, and then proceed to look at the nature of group effectiveness, and the role that communication processes play in achieving that effectiveness.

TEAMS: THE SPORTS METAPHOR

When talking about work teams, the temptation to use sporting analogies or metaphors is almost irresistible.[19] Most of us first encounter the word 'team' in a sporting setting, and it is only logical we should project our experience and perception of sporting teams onto work teams. While there are undoubtedly some illuminating comparisons to be drawn,[20] we should be careful about extending the analogy, or metaphor, because the dissimilarities between work teams and sporting teams tend to outweigh the similarities (see table 1.4).

Thus, work teams and sporting teams are similar in that they both share a *need to train and prepare* before going into action, and they also share a *need to coordinate and communicate* when action is underway.

Both types of teams can benefit from *goal-setting*, which can not only lay a logical basis for planning but can also be a motivator. ('Why are we trying so hard? *That's* why we're trying so hard!')

A coach can use *exhortation* to lift the morale of a sports team with a rallying speech, psyching up the players so they will try just that much harder; a leader or manager of a team can, under the right circumstances, obtain similar improvements in performance with the right kind of inspirational or visionary speech or conversation or memo.

Finally, being within a team — sporting or working — where everyone is working together harmoniously, in unison, can be a very pleasant experience, and that experience is enhanced further when the team experiences *synergy*, or that state where the collective output jumps above the mere sum of the individual outputs.

Table 1.4: Similarities and dissimilarities between work teams and sports teams

Similarities	Dissimilarities
• Both have a need for training and preparation. • Coordination and communication are important. • Goal-setting is needed for motivation and planning. • Exhortation can produce excitement, which can lead to better performance. • Working in unison, and experiencing synergy effects, can be very gratifying.	• Goals are clear in sport teams; not always clear/may be multiple/contradictory/in work teams. • In sport, it is unlikely that an individual can pursue goals separate from the team; at work, it is possible (albeit undesirable). • Exhortation can wear a bit thin in work situations. • Time-frames are limited in sport; sometimes open-ended, multiple at work. • Rules are known in sport; rules can be official and unofficial at work. • It is a stable information environment in sport: the future is reasonably predictable; turbulent information environment at work: future is not always predictable. • Physical effort is crucial in sport; at work, mental effort only, or mainly, is increasingly the case. • Aggression is channelled in sport; at work, overt aggression is usually inappropriate. • Sports teams are an end in themselves (entertainment); work teams are a means to an end (products, services). • Sports teams are collectively competitive; work teams are collaborative with other work teams. • Sports teams are usually culturally homogenous; work teams are often culturally heterogeneous.

(Adapted with permission from Eunson (1987); additional material from Collier (1992).)

The dissimilarities between sporting and work teams are, however, numerous. While they are clear in sporting teams, for example, *goals are not always clear* in working teams, and indeed there may be multiple and contradictory goals within and between work teams. Organisations are rarely unitary structures where everyone pulls together, laudable as that end might be. It is more realistic to see organisations as pluralistic coalitions of forces and empires, or as a double structure comprising the formal organisation on the one hand, which communicates through official channels, and the informal organisation on the other hand, which communicates through the grapevine. The goals of these sub-organisations do coincide — sometimes often, but rarely always.

Also, in sporting teams it is quite difficult for an individual to have goals different from the team and to remain inside that team; in work teams, however, people's actions and intentions are less transparent, more opaque, and it is possible for a non-conforming individual to have *separate goals* and yet stay inside the team. This is not always a good thing, but as we shall see later on, it *can* be a good thing, if it means resisting and challenging pressure to conform.

'Get out there and kill 'em — I know you can do it!' is fine in the locker room, and sometimes fine in the office or on the factory floor, but unless it is backed up with resources to do the job, and rewards upon completion of the job, *exhortation is not enough*, and wears thin very quickly.

In the workplace, *time-frames, rules and the information environment can be complex, ambiguous and unpredictable* — unlike the tidy realities of the playing field.

While the psychological game is increasingly important in sport, it is only so as a means to the end of improving physical performance. Yet the industrial revolutions of the past few centuries have meant that, in many workplaces, *physical labour is irrelevant*: it has been substantially replaced in many jobs by mental or intellectual labour, and it is quite difficult to know if the brain is sweating.

Similarly, aggression is normal within sport, and is usually kept under control within ritualised channels; in the workplace, however, *aggression is usually inappropriate* and its crudity as a force can be disastrously counter-productive, even when focused on outsiders like competitors.[21]

Sports teams are an end in themselves — they are primarily about entertainment, and it is not always vital that they win because of this. Work teams, in contrast, are merely *a means to an end*, namely, the production of products and services, and the consequences of 'losing' much or all of the time are far more serious.

Aggression and competition are closely linked. Sports teams are collectively competitive, in that they compete with other teams in the same league or table or system. The name of the game for work teams, however, is to be *collaborative, not competitive* with other teams in their organisation, not compete with them.

Finally, it is fairly common for sports teams to be culturally homogenous, in terms of gender, age and race. Such homogeneity is seen less and less in the real world of work, where *cultural heterogeneity* is more likely.

1. Ask three or four people to complete the team performance questionnaire and diagram. Discuss your experience with theirs.

2. Consider two organisations — they might be ones with which you are familiar, or ones with which your friends or family are familar. Where do they stand in the 'yesterday's organisation/tomorrow's organisation?' model (table 1.1)? What would their pyramid profiles look like?

3. Under what circumstances might the traditional bureaucratic organisation — 'yesterday's organisation' — be successful?

4. Table 1.2 lists various change factors in modern organisations. Can you think of any others?

5. Table 1.3 lists various pros and cons of teams. Can you think of any others?

6. How might work analogies or metaphors be used in sports teams?

- -

TALKING POINTS

YOU DON'T SAY? What people say about groups and teams

No man is an island, entire of itself ... every man is a piece of the continent, a part of the main; if a clod be washed away by the sea, Europe is the less, as well as if a promontary were, as well as if a manor of thy friends or of thine own were; any man's death diminishes me, because I am involved in mankind; and therefore never send to know for whom the bell tolls; it tolls for thee.

John Donne

Every man is an island.

Michael Leunig

Tell me with whom thou goest, and I'll tell thee what thou doest.

English proverb

Hell is other people.

Jean-Paul Sartre

Please accept my resignation. I don't care to belong to any club that will have me as a member.

Groucho Marx

Man is a knot, a web, a mesh into which relationships are tied. Only those relationships matter.

Antoine de Saint-Exupery

It is always possible to bind together a considerable number of people in love, so long as there are other people left over to receive the manifestations of their aggressiveness.

Sigmund Freud

When elderly invalids meet with fellow-victims of their own ailments, then at last real conversation begins, and life is delicious.

Logan Pearsall Smith

Cough and the world coughs with you. Fart and you fart alone.

Trevor Griffiths

With three or more people there is something bold in the air: direct things get said which would frighten two people alone and conscious of each inch of their nearness to one another. To be three is to be in public, you feel safe.

Elizabeth Bowen

In the hateful, hostile mob (O strange vagary!)
My only port and refuge can I find,
Such is my fear to find myself alone.

Petrarch

A wise man associating with the vicious, becomes an idiot; a dog travelling with good men becomes a rational being.

Arabic proverb

That I am totally devoid of sympathy for, or interest in, the world of groups is directly attributable to the fact that my two greatest needs — smoking cigarettes and plotting revenge — are basically solitary pursuits.

Fran Lebowitz

To associate with other like-minded people in small purposeful groups is for the great majority of men and women a source of profound psychological satisfaction. Exclusiveness will add to the pleasure of being several; and secrecy will intensify it almost to ecstasy.

Aldous Huxley

... the single biggest killer of teams is the lack of clear and honest communication between the team members.

Darrel W. Ray

Men strengthen each other in their faults. Those who are like associate together. Repeat the things which all believe, and stimulate their common faults of disposition, and each one receives from the other a reflection of his own egotism.

Henry Ward Beecher

We are half-ruined by conformity, but we should be wholly ruined without it.

Charles Dudley Warner

2

GROUP DYNAMICS

WHY GROUPS?

The group is the mechanism that links the individual to organisations and to society at large. It consists of people who feel they belong together and are united in a common purpose.

We are all members of numerous groups. Some of these groups are officially constituted, while others are more unofficial, informal, less obvious — but no less influential upon our behaviour for all of that.

Take a typical individual like Mary, for example. At work, Mary is a member of at least three groups (see figure 2.1), although she is the only person who is a member of all three groups shown.

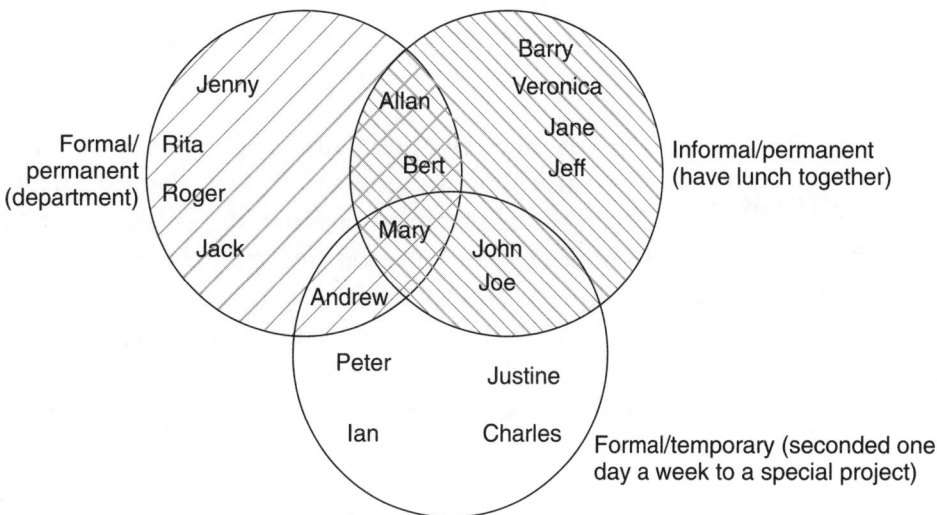

Figure 2.1: Group membership patterns

(Adapted from Hodgetts, 1980. Reproduced with permission from Eunson (1987).)

Mary may behave differently in all three group settings, or she may be the same in all of them. A diagram of all the groups Mary belongs to — her family, her softball team, her church congregation, the friends she goes out with on Saturday night — could get rather complicated. It would, nevertheless, comprise something of a map of identity of Mary; it would give us many clues as to her behaviour, values and opinions.

Groups, then, are vital to our understanding of the individual, and indeed, of society. But why do people join groups in the first place?

WHY DO PEOPLE JOIN GROUPS? WHY DO THEY STAY? WHY DO THEY LEAVE?

There are (at least) five reasons why people join, stay in or leave groups. These are:
1. security
2. task complexity
3. social interaction
4. propinquity
5. exchange.

1. Security

There is safety in numbers. Being a member of a group may make us feel more secure in a hostile environment and thus satisfy our security needs. United we stand, divided we fall.

2. Task complexity

Primitive humans joined together in groups or bands not only to satisfy security needs but also because only within the group could complex tasks be achieved: an individual might be able to trap a small animal or gather a small amount of plants, but to trap a big animal or gather a large amount of plants required the coordinated efforts of a group.

In modern work environments, groups are almost totally unavoidable: there are very few jobs that can be done by one isolated individual, such as, for example, a lighthousekeeper — and even then, such an individual is dependent upon a network of individuals and groups in the outside world to support such a solitary role.

3. Social interaction

People need people. Many people would dislike being a lighthousekeeper because they are gregarious, being social creatures rather than isolates. One of the greatest punishments within prison is to be placed in solitary confinement. A person may find the people he works with not all that inspiring, and then, one day, he wins the lottery. He quits the job, to take up a life of leisure. But unless he has other individuals and groups to interact with, to talk to, to gossip with, to laugh with, then life might get rather lonely. Ask five people who are in employment this question: if you won a million dollars tomorrow, would you quit your job? If any of them say no, then they may well be expressing the fact that they have fairly high social interaction needs, and that their current job satisfies a number of those needs.

4. Propinquity

Why do we choose to become members of one group, or set of groups, rather than others? Often, there is no reason in particular: we would possibly be just as happy in one group, or set of groups, or indeed culture, as another. The historical accident of geographical closeness — nearness, or propinquity — is a significant factor in the formation and duration over time of many groups. Thus you are more likely to interact with people you sit near to — at work, at school, at a sporting or cultural event — than with people you sit at a distance from.

5. Exchange

The exchange theory of group membership could best be summed up in the phrase: 'What's in it for me?' In other words, exchange theorists argue that we all — consciously or unconsciously — weigh up the costs and benefits of being in a group:

> *As long as what the person is getting from being a member of the group (friendship, support, satisfaction) exceeds the cost of being a member (time expended, favours given), he or she will remain a member.*[1]

EXERCISE

**B:
YOU AND THE GROUPS
YOU BELONG TO**

Now that we are aware of five factors which determine whether we join, stay in or leave groups, we can visually analyse our membership in different groups. Using a pie chart, we can — approximately — give differing proportions or weight to the segments of the pie showing the differing factors. For example, Mary could show the patterns of her membership of two groups like this:

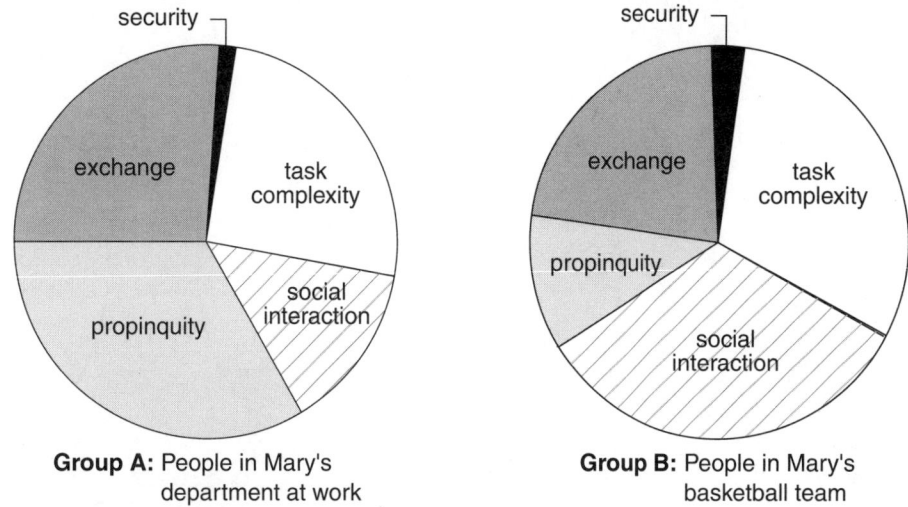

Group A: People in Mary's
department at work

Group B: People in Mary's
basketball team

Figure 2.2: Patterns of membership of two of Mary's groups

The factors are different for each group. If people or circumstances changed in either group, the diagram for that group would be different.

Your groups

Think of some groups you belong to. These might be:
- a work group
- the same work group two years ago
- a group of friends at school
- a group with which you socialise
- a sporting team
- your family.

Refer to the definitions of the five factors of group membership (security, task complexity, social interaction, propinquity and exchange), and then complete the blank pie graphs overleaf (figure 2.3), giving the segments of each pie their right size.

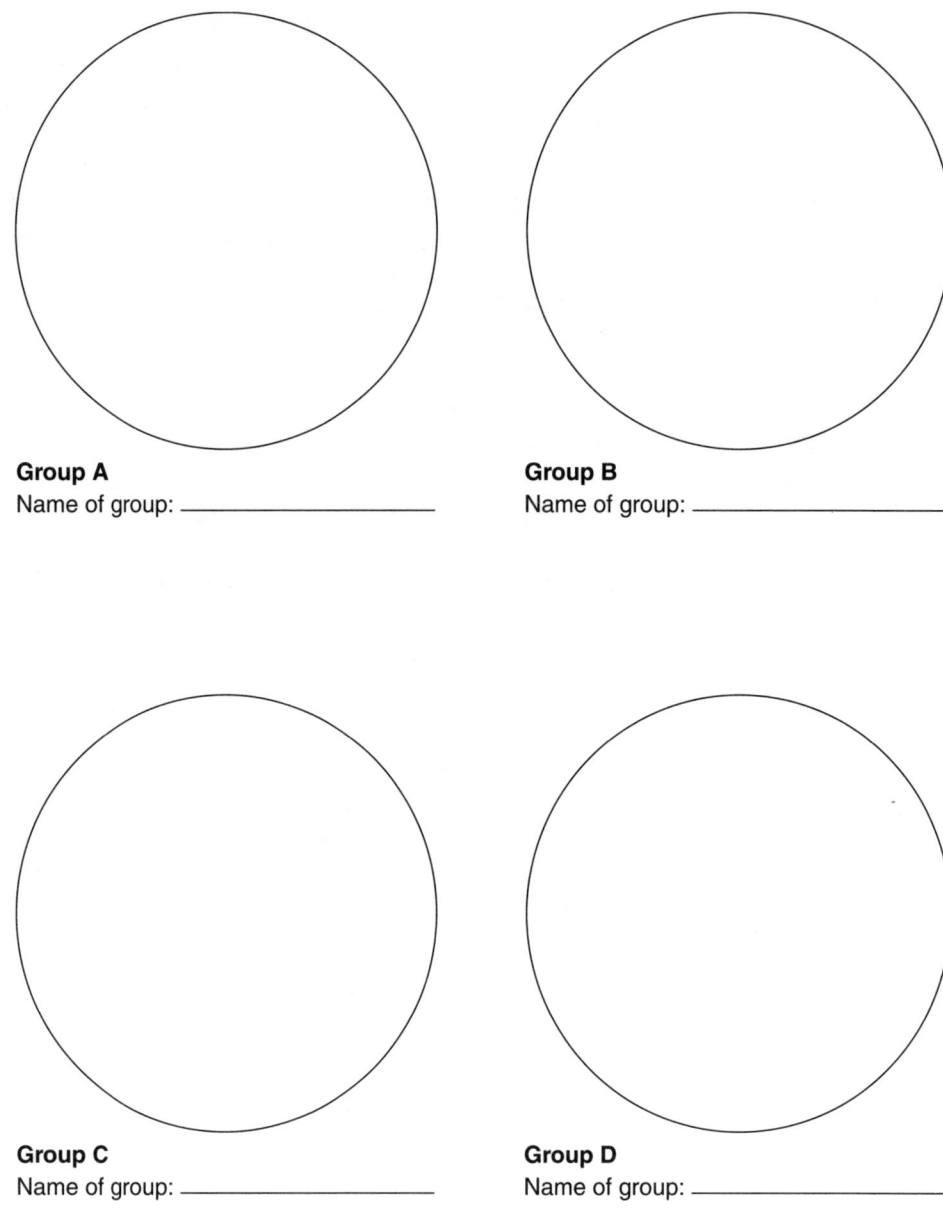

Group A
Name of group: _____

Group B
Name of group: _____

Group C
Name of group: _____

Group D
Name of group: _____

Figure 2.3: Patterns of membership of four of my groups

GROUP VERSUS INDIVIDUAL PERFORMANCE

We now have a fair idea of why people join, leave or stay in groups. But who is better at getting things done — groups or individuals? It's clear that when a task requires that many things be done at the same time, a group will be better than an individual. When a task requires that many things be done — but not necessarily at the same time — then the evidence is mixed: sometimes groups are better, sometimes individuals are.

The presence of others can produce results that would be better than those produced if we were operating alone: for example, an experiment conducted in 1897 showed that cyclists performed better when competing against other cyclists than when each cyclist simply competed against the clock — against themselves, in other words.[2]

The presence of others can have the opposite effect, however. When someone is 'looking over your shoulder', it seems all too easy to get something wrong, particularly when you are working on something new. Research suggests that when tasks are familiar, other people around us may cause us to perform better, but when tasks are unfamiliar, other people around us may cause us to perform worse.[3]

Synergy and social loafing

When a group experiences *synergy*, then its whole is greater than the sum of its parts. That is, the output of the group is higher and/or better than would have been the case if we had simply kept the group members apart from each other and added up their individual performances.[4]

The whole of the group can sometimes be less than the sum of its parts, however. Experiments with tug-of-war teams of different sizes showed that as group size increased, effort per person decreased. Similarly, individuals being secretly measured on their efforts at applause were found to clap harder as individuals or in small groups than in big groups. This effect, known as *social loafing*, may help to explain why some people's performance in groups — particularly where their individual output cannot be clearly measured — is lower than if they were working alone.[5]

Good or bad performance within groups is best understood in terms of the interplay of a number of factors, specifically roles, norms, status, cohesiveness and conformity, leadership, individual differences, and communication and problem-solving skills. Let's look at these in detail.

ROLES

Let's look first at T. M. Newcomb's definition of a group:[6]

A GROUP CONSISTS OF PEOPLE WITH SHARED NORMS AND INTERLOCKING ROLES.

A role can be defined as a set of activities expected of a person holding a particular office or position in a group or an organisation.[7] There are at least three different types of roles that people play in work groups:
1. task
2. socio-emotional
3. destructive.

Task roles are played by people when they are concerned solely with getting the job done. People playing different task roles might be of greater use to the team at different phases of a team's work pattern. Thus looking at the task roles listed in table 2.1, we can see that it

would make sense for a team to allow a creative person to start the team's work, and a recording person to finish it, with others contributing their special talents along the way. When we say that a particular person is adopting a particular task role, then we are considering them and their work from a functional viewpoint. We are more concerned with the quality and quantity of their output than we are with their feelings, values and opinions.

Socio-emotional roles are played by people when they are communicating feelings, values and opinions about the task, and about the world beyond the task. They are sometimes also known as maintenance roles, because they are concerned with the maintenance of the human dimension of teamwork.

Destructive roles are played by people when they — consciously or unconsciously — wish to sabotage the efforts of the group.

Table 2.1 lists names given to these sets of roles in the work group.

Table 2.1: Names given to the roles people play in work groups

Task roles	Socio-emotional roles	Destructive roles
Brainstormer	Encourager	Husher
Expert	Peacemaker	Personaliser
Judge	Tension-reliever	Recognition-seeker
Devil's advocate	Confronter	Victim
Representative		Blocker
Implementer		Shelver
Chairperson		Distractor
Secretary/note-taker		Aggressor
		Shadow
		Special interest pleader

More detailed analysis of these types of roles played within groups — in terms of their verbal, non-verbal and general behaviour — can be found in table 2.2.

The key to role effectiveness in groups is to ensure that members strike a good balance in playing task roles and socio-emotional roles, and to ensure that there is an absolute minimum of destructive role-playing. Too much emphasis on task roles may lead to an over-emphasis on facts, and not enough weight given to opinion and feeling (which can be as important, and sometimes more important, than facts). Too much emphasis on socio-emotional roles may lead to a too-extreme de-emphasis of facts and not enough concern with producing real outcomes from the group.

Table 2.2: Analysis of roles within groups

TASK ROLES			
Role	**Verbal behaviour**	**Non-verbal behaviour**	**Analysis**
Brainstormer	• Hey, what about . . . • I'm really excited about . . . • No, don't judge, not yet anyway. • We've possibly got ourselves into this mess because we're too conventional /tired/ boring. • We're too close to it: we need lateral thinking here, not vertical.	• jumps up, writes on board/flip chart • jerky, explosive movements • animated face, eyes • touches others	• invaluable when team needs new ideas, i.e., all the time • not necessarily good at execution, i.e., a starter, not a finisher • possibly a short concentration span • might be disorganised • good at finding things and concepts — good at losing them, too • might need to have creativity channelled via structure, goals — ask for ideas in writing where possible • may need to be protected from more 'practical' members of team
Expert	• Here are the facts/data. • My presentation begins with . . . • I presume you've all read my report/memo on . . . • Let's stick to the facts.	• serious, methodical, restrained • precise hand gestures — folds hands, points at diagrams, charts • slightly impatient waiting to be asked to go into action	• not emotional • thinks the pure beauty of ideas is obvious to everyone • impatient with politics — doesn't understand compromise, lobbying, or the necessity to repeat a good idea consistently • may be intolerant of Brainstormer's 'messiness', emotional communication
Judge	• We've got conflicting opinions here. • Let's weigh up the pros and cons. • Where's the practicality/ logic? • Maybe we should sleep on it, and look at it later — it might benefit from some benign neglect. • Maybe we should put together a compromise package of parts of all proposals.	• evaluative, e.g., biting glasses arm /pen, narrowing of eyes, chin-stroking • laying-down-law type of hand-chop • counting on fingers in discussing alternatives • gestures with one hand, then the other ('on the one hand . . . and on the other . . .')	• can work with Experts from differing fields • might be an enemy of Brainstormer by forcing premature closure on decisions

(continued)

Table 2.2: Analysis of roles within groups (*continued*)

TASK ROLES			
Role	**Verbal behaviour**	**Non-verbal behaviour**	**Analysis**
Devil's advocate	• I can see a lot of good here, but let's look at it from the opposition's point of view. • Do we have any blind spots here? • What's the worst-case scenario? What can go horribly wrong? Let's not forget Murphy's Law.	• sits back in chair — remains restrained even when ideas are flying and enthusiasm is high • takes notes	• necessary to prevent Groupthink syndrome (see p. 42) • vital that this role be rotated, otherwise there is the danger of Advocate simply becoming a Blocker
Representative	• The unions/management won't like parts of this. • I'll make a few calls. • I'll do some press releases, take X and Y to lunch and give them some background.	• shares similar behaviour of Judge, Devil's Advocate and Implementer (evaluation, detachment, alertness)	• a liaison with outside interests and stakeholders • a boundary-spanner • a negotiator, a fixer • might have divided loyalties
Implementer	• Can do. • Sure. • Okay. • I'll have a draft back to this group in a week. • There are ways and means. • Leave it to me.	• alert • shuffles, arranges papers • makes notations, uses highlighter pen • looks at watch • writes in diary • uses calculator/laptop computer	• a master of details • a fixer • can become impatient, however, and might force team to premature closure
Chairperson	• That's quite interesting, X, but I think we'll handle it as a separate item under general business on the agenda. • We seem to have reached an impasse: let me see if I can summarise the differing viewpoints we've heard so far. • That's out of line, Y — please stick to discussing item 6, otherwise A and B can have the floor.	• works through agenda papers with pen • often has hand over mouth while others are speaking • looks around table to watch for cues indicating who would like to speak • confers with secretary/note-taker	• ideally, should have no strong opinions on matters under discussion (perfect neutrality is, of course, impossible) • it is useful to know his/her real opinions in case a casting vote is needed
Secretary/note-taker	• Excuse me Y, how do you spell that? • Silence	• head down	• the collective memory and handler of mechanics — minutes, agendas, checking up to see that people have followed through on items on last agenda

SOCIO-EMOTIONAL ROLES			
Role	**Verbal behaviour**	**Non-verbal behaviour**	**Analysis**
Encourager	• Before we go any further, I think we should hear from X. She's been giving me some opinions, and I think there's a lot in them. X? The floor is yours. • No, No, I don't think that's what X meant at all. I think she was saying . . . . Have I got that right, X, or have I missed your point?	• smile, nod • head tilted to one side; listening • open palms	• draws out reticent, and protects the weak • supports Chairperson • a good listener
Peacemaker	• Let's go back a few steps, J.: you agree that . . . , right? And S., you also agree that . . . , right? • Yes, I understand that you disagree with . . . but my notes show that you agree with . . . . Okay?	• orients towards person with hot temper • gestures towards them (palms open, up) • appealing, soothing • eyebrows up (questioning)	• consensus-seeker, diplomat — knows there may be no permanent solution to the problem under discussion • knows that tempers may cool if team takes a break; may thus propose adjournment when conflict peaks
Tension-reliever	• Uses puns, jokes • Time for coffee/lunch, I think. • Hey, I didn't know World War III had been declared.	• pulls faces • smiles, laughs • animated face, body • expansive gestures • plays with pens, cups • doodles	• good at breaking the ice in initial phases of team meetings • good at defusing conflict with humour • needs to know how not to go too far, otherwise clowning will irritate people, and be counterproductive • similar to Brainstormer, but not as creative in transforming facts into ideas
Confronter	• No, we can't smoothe this over. • There's a hidden agenda here; there's too many undercurrents in this group. We need to get this out in the open before we go any further. • No, I disagree — we shouldn't just stick to the facts. Facts can be twisted to suit any opinion. We need opinions, and we need honest opinions — no more playing games.	• assertive/aggressive manner • shakes head • palm out in 'stop' gesture • negative cross-fanning of hands	• more assertive than aggressive • not all conflict is bad: the Confronter is useful when conflict is being avoided, when team pussyfoots around hard decisions • enemy of 'weak' consensus, i.e., taking the path of least resistance • similar to Devil's advocate, except that Confronter is more concerned with opinions and feelings than facts

(continued)

Table 2.2: Analysis of roles within groups (*continued*)

DESTRUCTIVE ROLES			
Role	**Verbal behaviour**	**Non-verbal behaviour**	**Analysis**
Husher	• Tsk, tsk. • Shh. • Let's not have any more of this unpleasantness. • I'm getting a headache.	• rapid head nods • palms out, palms down — calming, hushing, placating gestures • nervous posture • squirms • sickly smile • head-shaking • index finger to lips, and reprimanding, negating gestures • blushing	• wishes to avoid conflict at all costs • the appearance of harmony is all-important to the Husher • unwittingly aids other, more manipulative types in suppressing real discussion
Personaliser	• This is a roundabout way of attacking me, isn't it? • Why are you always attacking stuff from my area? • Humphh!	• hands to chest, thumb to chest • higher pitch in voice • wide open, staring eyes • crossed arms, body orientated away from group after outburst	• alternates between aggressive/fight and submissive/flight behaviour • feels that world is out to get him/her: the most innocent remarks from others are seen as an attack upon the Personaliser's self, home department, ethnic group, religion • if this is continued long enough, the perceived will become the real; paranoia will become objective. People will perceive such a person in a different way, and therefore will behave differently towards them
Recognition seeker	• It's funny that this should come up, you know. Something similar, well, not quite similar, happened to me about two years ago. I wrote about it in my half-yearly report — I'm sure you all remember? • Loud laughter, drawing people's attention and stopping discussion. • You know, we've been working on this for quite some time in my section. Let me fill you in.	• self-confident, smug • suddenly leans forward at point of interruption • fidgets • may be flamboyant in dress	• has a short concentration span • is bored with most things, especially when he or she is not the centre of attention • similar to the Personaliser, in that he or she insists on relating the most unrelated matters back to him/herself; unlike the Personaliser, however, the Recognition-seeker is quite happy about this

	DESTRUCTIVE ROLES		
Role	**Verbal behaviour**	**Non-verbal behaviour**	**Analysis**
Victim	• I've really mucked this one up. Anyone got any bright ideas? • Sorry, I guess I've let the team down again. • We're just crumpling under pressure down in my section. We can't cope. • It's a no-win situation — again.	• drooping, slumped posture • peaked eyebrows, wrinkled brow • shakes head • entwines, disentwines legs • appeals to others with eyes, hands	• everyone fails from time to time — at least a mistake indicates that someone stopped talking long enough to do something. The Victim, however, fails all the time, apparently having made the life-decision that if praise is not available, then disapproval, or even punishment, is okay. Victims eventually get their wish. • a type of masochistic Recognition-seeker
Blocker	• It'll never work. • What a mess! • I don't know why we bother. • It's never been done before. • We tried that before, and it didn't work. • It can't happen under the 1961 standing orders, and therefore it's not *gonna* happen.	• crossed arms • theatrical sighs • contemptuous looks • rolls eyes • shakes head • orientates body away	• has one way to say 'yes', and a million ways to say 'no' — a nay-sayer • negative and destructive in approach: everything is a problem • enamoured of red tape • Confronter/Devil's Advocate gone wrong
Shelver	• Shouldn't we defer this? • Is this the best place to discuss this? • I don't know, I still think we need more information.	• whining voice • very worried looks • looks at watch/clock • looks as though he or she wants to be somewhere else	• a procrastinator and an avoider • sometimes delaying things can be wise, but the Shelver always wants to put things off • less aggressive than the Blocker, but just as effective in frustrating action
Distractor	• Whispers a lot. • Psst! • Anyway, she said . . . he said . . .	• passes notes • winks • nudges • yawns • looks everywhere but at agenda	• short concentration span • treats all meetings as social occasions • doesn't necessarily want to be elsewhere, because a lot of gossip items may come up here • similar to Recognition-seeker in producing terminally trivial and silly behaviour but does not want so high a profile

(continued)

Table 2.2: Analysis of roles within groups (*continued*)

DESTRUCTIVE ROLES			
Role	**Verbal behaviour**	**Non-verbal behaviour**	**Analysis**
Aggressor	• God! What a lot of garbage you're talking! • That's typical of the gutless, incompetent nonsense we've come to expect of you! • What kickback are *you* going to get from this? • Tsk, tsk, tsk.	• glares • bares teeth • points • shakes fist • crosses arms • shakes head • broad, dismissive gestures • loud exhalation of air, expressing disgust	• very hostile • suspicious of people's motives • dominates, and often wins
Shadow	• Says nothing.	• sits back from table • frightened or impassive	• is not quite clear why he or she is there • may have some good things to say, but is dominated by others • needs an Encourager, or needs to be taken off the team
Special interest pleader	• Yes, all very well, but what about the small businessman/ poor/ housewives/ big companies staggering under the tax burden/ data-processing department?	• sermonising tone of voice • looks intently around table at others while talking	• draws all topics back to special interest, no matter how irrelevant the connection may be • the Representative gone wrong • the Personaliser operating at a collective level

TALKING POINTS

IDENTIFYING ROLES: THE SOCIOGRAM

Another approach to identifying roles played within groups is to use sociogram analysis.

The sociogram in figure 2.4 represents a group of twelve students in a college, each circle representing an individual student. Each student was asked the following question:

If you had to be on a committee of four members including yourself, who else (if anyone) would you choose to work with you? You may choose three people but, clearly, you don't have to nominate three, just those with whom you would most like to work. Also identify those people (if any) with whom you would dislike working. You may identify three people you would least prefer to work with, but you don't have to.

In the sociogram, the *positive choices* (most preferred) are represented by black lines, while the *negative choices* (least preferred) are represented by broken lines.

Social relationships, typical of most groups, are shown in this sociogram. Usually, two personality characteristics are revealed by sociograms: popularity and isolation.

1. Popularity

Four choice patterns are associated with a popular personality:

(a) *The star*: The most popular person, or the star, receives the most votes. In our sociogram, No. 5 is the star, because he receives six votes out of a possible eleven.

(b) *Mutually attractive pair*: This refers to reciprocating friendship choices, such as Nos 7 and 8.

(c) *Chain structures*: These are the friendship structures that link individuals in a chain form. The chain series can either be reciprocal or unreciprocal choices. Numbers 8, 7, 6, 3 and 2 form a reciprocal chain.

(d) *The clique*: This is the trio that forms a triangle like Nos 3, 4 and 6 forms a closed friendship group — that is, each member chooses, and is chosen by, the other two.

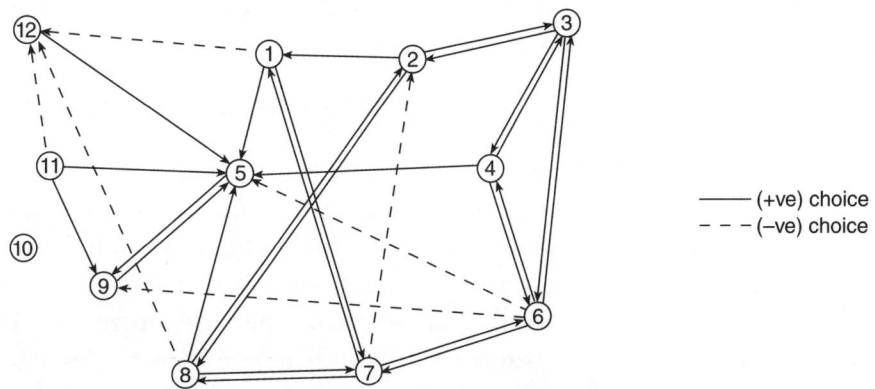

Figure 2.4: Sociogram of twelve college students
(Source: Teasedale (1976: 214–16). Reproduced with permission.)

2. Isolation

Three variables of isolation are often presented in the structure of a group:

(a) *The rejectee*: No. 12 is rejected by Nos 1, 8 and 11, but is not chosen by anyone: in fact, he is rejected.

(b) *The neglectee*: No. 11 is not rejected by anyone, but is not chosen by anyone either. He is ignored and neglected.

(c) *The isolate*: The term 'isolate' describes the person who neither makes a choice nor receives a choice. In our sociogram, No. 10 is an isolate.

A final choice pattern emerges which is frequently referred to as the *power behind the throne*. Number 9 is an example of the power behind the throne for, although he is chosen only once, this choice is by the star, and he can be characterised as having considerable influence within the group in an indirect way.

1. What are the strengths and weaknesses of the various roles within a group?
2. What is the ideal balance of task and socio-emotional roles?
3. How might a chairperson best control Destructive role players?
4. To what extent should a chairperson play some or all of the Socio-emotional roles?
5. Are the roles that people play an expression of deep-seated and unchangeable character, or are they more superficial than this?
6. Do people play more than one role in the same group? Do they play different roles in different groups?
7. What other roles might there be?
8. Sociograms can reveal some uncomfortable realities in groups. If you were a consultant working with the group whose sociogram is shown in figure 2.4, how would you try and improve the group's effectiveness?

NORMS

You may recall that our working definition of a group is that it consists of people with shared norms and interlocking roles. Norms are the rules or standards of behaviour we expect from others and from ourselves. If you like, 'norms' can be translated as 'rules'. Thus a good way to define groups is:

ROLES + RULES (NORMS) = GROUPS

What do norms look like? If you look at the questionnaire in Exercise A, (p. 2), you will see various norms as they apply to groups or teams — norms of motivation and goals, communication and feedback, status and power, team effectiveness, and decision-making and problem-solving. We can also make a distinction between formal norms and informal norms in work groups. Formal norms are those rules that are explicit in the way they define the group's behaviour; informal norms are implicit in the way they define the group's behaviour.

An example of a factory work group's formal and informal norms are shown in table 2.3.

Table 2.3: Formal and informal norms as they relate to a factory work group[8]

Formal norms	Informal norms
Workers show up at the factory on time.	Workers often refer to each other by nicknames.
Workers must observe safety regulations.	Some workers engage in practical jokes and horseplay.
Workers in this group have lunch in the cafeteria from 12: 45 to 1: 30 p.m.	Workers in this group always sit at the one table and always drink three cups of coffee.

In workplaces, formal norms tend to be set up and enforced by management, whereas informal norms tend to be set and enforced by the work group of peers. Such informal norms can be negative and punitive, or positive and rewarding. All have the unstated function of preserving the group and its collective self-esteem.

If anyone deviates from these norms — fails to conform, in other words — they are usually punished by various group behavioural mechanisms, such as ostracism ('sent to Coventry', 'freeze out') or ridicule ('Ratebuster!', 'Conch!' for over-achievers, 'Goldbricker!', 'Bludger!' for under-achievers).

TALKING POINTS **GROUP PRESSURE AND THE ENFORCEMENT OF NORMS**

Informal friendship groups occur most often across the hierarchy — peers, rather than bosses and subordinates, are friends. It is true that in very loose, open hierarchies, different hierarchical levels do form friendship groups, but this is still the exception rather than the rule.

The influence of the friendship group is greatest at the base of the hierarchy, where relationships between members are the strongest.

Conversely, members at the top of the hierarchy do have informal relationships, but there is little friendship involved; senior managers' informal relationships are based on convenience rather than love.

The power of groups to affect the behaviour of members should not be underestimated. People are affected by groups throughout their daily lives — in work groups, committees, families or friendship groups. The ultimate control of the group is total rejection, a form of isolation few can endure for long.

This process of influencing behaviour in groups can be traced. When a deviation from the expected behaviour occurs, phases of control will be seen.

Phase 1: initial tolerance

The deviation is noted by the members of the group. They may seek an explanation ('Why are you doing that, Harry?') or members may make excuses ('She hasn't learnt the ropes yet.') Whatever the technique (and it may be total silence), members of the group have registered the deviation and the implied message is: 'Okay, we note the deviation. Now let's be sensible and not deviate.'

Phase 2: attempt at correction

Members have noted the continued deviation from group norms and deliberately attempt to correct the behaviour. 'Don't keep doing that,' 'Put your clothes back on again,' 'You don't have to go home yet,' 'Have another beer,' and so on. At this stage, members of the group are still tolerant, but are signalling verbally or non-verbally that the deviation must cease.

Phase 3: verbal aggression

Other group members are becoming more annoyed by the deviation. Verbal messages become more hostile, or more aggressive, and the threat of rejection may be offered: 'If you can't do it this way, don't do it at all,' (fail and go elsewhere). Verbal aggression is more likely to occur than physical aggression in groups whose members come from middle- or upper-income families. Lower-income groups use more physical aggression.

Phase 4: physical aggression

As a control, this is limited by other group norms (e.g., no physical aggression). It is more likely to be used on the factory floor than in the boardroom (where the process is often more subtle but no less damaging).

Phase 5: rejection ('Get out')

As soon as the individual is rejected (physically or psychologically), group members will rebalance power and roles, eliminate the deviant's contribution and, if necessary, readjust its norms. Probably the most frequently used rejection is total silence. In many cases, members of a group ignore all the niceties and reject immediately. Or the group may move from phase 2 to 5. In other words, the phases are sequential but not necessarily consecutive.

The power of the peer group has been known to managers and union officials for many years, and both use that power to influence the behaviour of employees. What is particularly different about work groups, as opposed to others, is that the norms and standards are central to the rewards the members receive. If a deviant decides to produce more than the group norm, then all members of the group are threatened. Similarly, if the employees feel industrial action is warranted, they will not tolerate non-conformists because non-conformists weaken the group's position. Work groups are very much a case of 'one in, all in'.

(Source: Hunt, John (1979) *Managing People at Work* (London: McGraw-Hill). Reproduced with permission.)

In 1948, a classic study was done of group norm behaviour in an American pyjama manufacturing plant.[9] At this plant, the informal group norm for productivity in a group of pressers was about fifty items a day. A new worker entered the group (see figure 2.5) and, after a few days' learning, began to exceed the group norm.

The rest of the group began to scapegoat or punish the newcomer deviating from the norm, so that after some days, the deviant conformed, and in fact over-conformed by producing slightly less than the group norm.

After twenty days, the group was split up. Other workers were transferred elsewhere, but the scapegoated worker remained. Her output rate increased dramatically, freed as she was from the restrictive group norm.

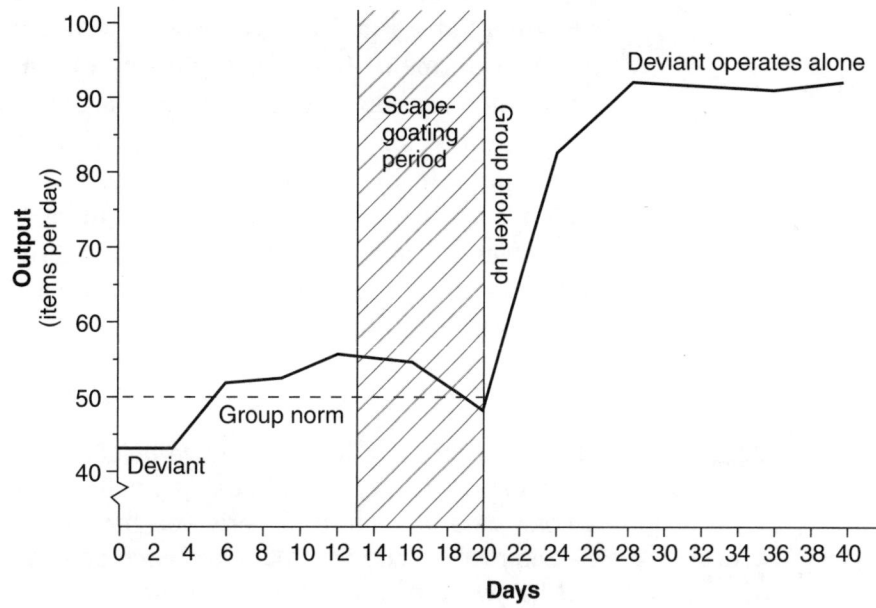

Figure 2.5: Group norms and deviant performance in a pyjama factory

(Source: Adapted from Coch and French, 1948. Reproduced with permission from Eunson (1987).)

Formal versus informal norms: trust and teams

What implications does this hold for teams? If teams are to maximise output, then negative informal norms have to be eliminated. But potentially negative formal norms have to be closely examined as well. For example, if team output goes up, does compensation/pay go up as well, or does it stay the same? If team output goes up, is there a chance that staff will be laid off if management perceives that it can produce the same amount with fewer people?[10]

It's a question of basic human motivation: people want to know, 'What's in it for me/us?' If the answer is something like: 'Your success (increased output) will be punished with dismissal,' it's hardly surprising that informal groups band together in self-defence to do less than they are capable of. Bland statements of the type, 'Restructuring has meant that we can do 10 per cent better with 30 per cent fewer people,' conceal a lot of heartbreak about the fate of the 30 per cent no longer there. The paradox with some workplace reforms, many of which use team-based production, is that norms of high productivity depend upon norms of high trust and open communication — qualities that are in short supply when there has been a bloodbath of 'downsizing' or 'reduction in force'. In tough economic times, of course, people need to try harder, but if people in departments and teams are so fearful that they might be the next to go, then fear drives out trust and openness, both within teams and between teams and management; this in turn drives out creativity and productivity, and the whole exercise becomes counter-productive. This is a game that no-one wins. Viewed in this light, informal group norms which hold down output seem almost like an oasis of civilisation.

The trick is to break out of such a dilemma, and see that the formal and informal norms of high productivity depend upon the formal and informal norms of high trust and open communication. Trust and communication are thus not luxuries (see section on 'trust', p. 72).

Similarly, all of the communication skills that enhance team-building which are considered in this book are not simply add-ons, or band-aids which cover gaping organisational wounds. If the commitment to openness from top management down is not genuine, then employees would be better off working in more authoritarian — but less hypocritical — traditional organisations.

EXERCISE

**C:
IDENTIFYING
NORMS**

Think of a group or team you have belonged to, or currently belong to. This might be a work group, a friendship group, a group you belonged to at school, a committee you sit on, a party you have attended, a queue or group in a waiting room, a sporting team, a church congregation, and so on.

What were or are the rules or norms, official and unofficial, of such a group? What did you have to do to get in, and to be accepted? What would you have to do to get out, and/or to be rejected? What was or is acceptable behaviour in terms of:

- clothing
- grooming
- language (e.g., special words or jargon which would exclude outsiders)
- non-verbal behaviour (e.g., secret signs, gestures)
- high performance (excelling)
- low performance (not trying hard)
- expression of emotions, feelings
- level of trust
- giving and receiving criticism?

How were or are norms expressed and enforced? In writing? In words? In looks, winks, rolling of eyes or other non-verbal behaviour? Analyse these norms by completing the chart opposite. Where possible, compare your analysis with those of other people.

NORM ANALYSIS CHART

Group: _____

	Norm	HOW EXPRESSED? HOW ENFORCED?		
		Written	Verbal	Non-verbal
Formal				
Informal				

NORMS OF COHESIVENESS AND CONFORMITY: GROUPTHINK AND THE ABILENE PARADOX

Conforming to or going along with norms can hold down or increase a group's output. The more conformity, the greater the cohesiveness or unity in the group. This is not always such a bad thing: while 'conformity' may sound undesirable to many, 'unity' sounds better to the same ears — yet the two concepts are merely two sides of the one coin.

Conformity to norms can also affect the quality of decision-making within groups. Social psychologist Irving Janis has argued that highly cohesive groups often make bad decisions because of a syndrome or behavioural trap he called 'groupthink'. The syndrome has eight symptoms as detailed in table 2.4.

Table 2.4: Symptoms of Groupthink

SYMPTOMS OF GROUPTHINK	
1. **Illusion of invulnerability**	The group believes it is invulnerable, which leads to excessive optimism and risk-taking.
2. **Rationalisation**	Group members rationalise away warnings or threats.
3. **Belief in inherent morality**	Group members believe that their decisions are inherently moral, brushing away thoughts of unethical behaviour by saying: 'How could *we* do anything wrong?'
4. **Stereotyping**	Opponents of the group are stereotyped as being too evil, stupid or weak to take seriously.
5. **Direct pressure**	Anyone foolhardy enough to question the status quo within the group has direct pressure applied to conform.
6. **Self-censorship**	Group members with doubts censor themselves to preserve the appearance of consent.
7. **Illusion of unanimity**	Because silence is interpreted as consent, there is an illusion of unanimity.
8. **Mind-guards**	Just as bodyguards protect us from physical harm, so some people set themselves as mind-guards or censors or gate-keepers in order to prevent challenging or threatening information available outside the group from appearing before the group.

(Adapted with permission from Eunson (1987).)

The paradox with Groupthink is that the groups it afflicts are usually quite pleasant company to work with — the 'we-feeling' is very high, and group members often like each other a lot. In fact, the more cohesive the group, the greater the chance of Groupthink occurring. The Groupthink model was originally used to explain foreign policy decision-making under various American presidents — Roosevelt (Pearl Harbour), Kennedy (Bay of Pigs, Cuban Missile Crisis), and Johnson (Vietnam).

It has also been applied to the Watergate crisis under Nixon[12] and, more recently, it has been applied to understanding the dynamics of the Falklands/Malvinas war of 1982 and the psychological mechanisms that could trigger a third world war.[13]

In 1961, for example, President Kennedy and his group of advisors made a bad decision to go ahead with supporting an invasion of Cuba at the Bay of Pigs by anti-Castro rebels. The invasion was a disaster. All the mechanisms of Groupthink contributed to this negative outcome — the perception the enemy was weak and incompetent, a norm of suppressing feelings, intuitions and criticism, a fear of being seen as weak if expressing criticism of the plan, dominance of the group by forceful, aggressive personalities such as Robert Kennedy, exclusion of alternative data, and so on.

The same group made better decisions in 1962 at the time of the Cuban missile crisis, employing a number of anti-Groupthink techniques (see table 2.5). Other decision-makers were brought into the group to provide fresh perspectives, President Kennedy deliberately excluded himself from some meetings so that his presence would not dominate and lead to suppression of ideas or self-censorship, and each person was sanctioned by the President to be a critical evaluator or devil's advocate of all ideas.

The Groupthink model was used in these studies to explain the behaviour of high-level political cabinets and ministries, but the model is just as useful in explaining the behaviour of a sporting team, a charity fundraising committee, a teenage gang or a work group.

A variation on the Groupthink model has been developed by Jerry Harvey, which he calls *The Abilene Paradox*.[14] The name comes from a journey Harvey and his family took through blistering heat to go to the town of Abilene, in Texas, to eat at a restaurant. Upon returning home, all four family members discovered that none of them really wanted to go, but each went along, presuming that everyone else wanted to go. In such circumstances, we make bad decisions, not so much due to actual group tyranny and conformity pressures, as to our own perceptions or anxiety about being alone, about being separated from others by exclusion or ostracism. Harvey notes, for example, that a number of President Nixon's staff who participated in the Watergate hotel break-in in 1972 didn't really want to do it, but thought that everyone else did: as one participant said: '(I) ... drifted along ... because of the fear of the group pressure that would ensue, of not being a team player ...'.

The Abilene Paradox is, then, 'Organisations frequently take actions in contradiction to what they really want to do and therefore defeat the very purposes they are trying to achieve.' The essential symptom that defines organisations caught in the paradox is that they are unable to manage agreement, rather than unable to manage conflict — because most agree with each other, rather than disagree, but all are operating in a fog of pluralistic ignorance.

How can Groupthink and the Abilene Paradox be avoided? There are numerous ways, most of which will be uncomfortable for group members, but some or all of which may be necessary. They are all basically concerned with expanding the focus of decision-making, reducing or modifying the cohesiveness of the group, and reducing the risk of speaking out within the group. These approaches are summarised in table 2.5.

Table 2.5: How to reduce the effects of Groupthink and the Abilene Paradox[15]

WAYS OF REDUCING GROUPTHINK AND THE ABILENE PARADOX	
1. **Examine alternatives, generate contingency plans**	Don't be trapped into thinking that there's only one solution: insist that multiple solutions be proposed for problems. Always have a Plan B, and preferably, a Plan C and Plan D.
2. **Appoint devil's advocate**	A devil's advocate is someone empowered by the group to always present a critical, worst-case-scenario view — without the group thinking any the worse of that person. Role needs to be rotated.
3. **Increase group size, heterogeneity**	Break the cosy dynamics — or statics — of the group by making it bigger, and introduce people who are from different backgrounds, opinions, problem-solving styles, who may challenge the consensus and expose the blind spots of an over-homogeneous group.
4. **Remove physical isolation**	Physically reintegrate group with the rest of the organisation — break down over-territorial 'us-and-them' mentality.
5. **Facilitate organisational graffiti**	Officially sanction space on organisational computer system for a graffiti bulletin board — people may anonymously input unpopular ideas and heresies so all might consider. Dangerous, but less dangerous than trying to suppress the grapevine.
6. **Eliminate competition with other groups**	Break down 'us–them' mentality by social occasions, forcing groups to work together, exchanging personnel between groups.
7. **Make confronters into heroes**	Going beyond the devil's advocate. Instead of shooting messengers, reward them. Very painful, but less painful than the alternative, which usually leads to someone saying: 'How did we get into this mess?' If assertively confronting role models exist, and are rewarded — or at the very least, are not punished — then there will be more assertive confrontation.
8. **Create multiple affiliations**	Have group members report to more than one boss, interact with other areas, departments, teams — expose them to other views, give them other supports they could fall back on if they fall out of favour with main group.

WAYS OF REDUCING GROUPTHINK AND THE ABILENE PARADOX	
9. **Establish multiple sub-groups to work on same problem**	Sub-groups will probably develop different approaches — presenting these back to the plenary group can be useful, as can the clashes which may occur between differing sub-groups and which may in turn produce yet more new approaches and insights into potential flaws.
10. **Create 'second chances'**	Hold 'second chance' meetings after consensus is apparently achieved on key issues.
11. **Use special techniques, e.g., nominal group technique**	Nominal group techniques (see p. 111) reduce group pressures to conform by allowing members to anonymously contribute ideas in writing.
12. **Have leaders absent themselves from some meetings.**	Leaders may 'freeze up' creatively by consciously or unconsciously creating norms of conformity.

TALKING POINTS

CASE STUDY: roles, norms and conformity

By noon Monday, Julia Costello was feeling stressed. The lone woman in the boardroom, she watched the enthusiastic discussion among the other managers with some alarm: she had wanted to generate enthusiasm, but she had not anticipated it would go in this direction.

As the newly-appointed human resources manager of Western Technologies Corporation, Julia had just completed a presentation to the Monday morning heads of department meeting on the subject of boosting productivity by changing group norms on the shop floor and in the accounts department.

The start of the presentation had been delayed while a loud and humorous discussion about Saturday's main football match had taken place. The managing director, Mike Johannson, was an ex-player in the main league, and he often brought videotapes of matches along and played them before the start of the meeting while people were drinking their first coffee of the day.

Football bored Julia, and she knew it bored at least two of the other managers present, but they certainly seemed to have a detailed knowledge of football trivia in this morning's banter.

Most of the managers were concerned with the production of WTC's main products, microprocessor-controlled gauges and monitoring equipment. Industrial relations between management and workers had not been good for quite some time. Indeed, a number of the managers referred to parts of the shop floor as 'sheltered workshops', and the standing joke addressed to Julia was that she was the 'inhuman' resources manager.

When Julia started talking, she was aware that not everyone was concentrating; there were winks, raised eyebrows and note-passing around the table. How childish, she thought. But after about five minutes, she noticed that Mike Johannson was looking less politely bored, and was beginning to take notes. Others began to do likewise.

Julia proposed that productivity levels could be raised by at least 15 per cent if she could get the go-ahead to start a team-building program, linked in with group bonuses of 1 per cent per 1.5 per cent productivity rise. Her brief, potted history of research in the area (not too much jargon, she hoped) gave evidence that it could be done.

'... and thus we could lift our market share and/or lower prices, as well as motivate staff more. It's a win-win situation', she concluded, and sat down.

Silence. There was some uncomfortable shifting in seats, and numerous unhappy faces. Max Rinter, the marketing manager, was the first to speak: 'That's good stuff, Julia, but ... I don't know about lowering prices. Our major client is the government, and they might start asking some embarrassing questions about why we couldn't have done this years ago. We could end up with egg on our faces.' Heads nodded around the table.

'What about increasing our output, Max?' asked Johansson.

'That could be tricky, too', said Rinter. 'The quota is pre-set, and if we try to move more, they might think we're being pushy. Inventory costs will go up if we try to stockpile in this part of the seasonal cycle.'

Jack Tuttle, the production manager, jumped in: 'That motivation stuff is interesting, Julia, but I'd need to re-jig the machines to get them working in groups. But I can see a lot of sense putting people onto piece rates to boost production.'

'What about the surplus goods, Jack?' Max said sarcastically.

'Surplus goods or surplus people?' responded Tuttle. 'If Julia's figures are correct, then according to the calculations I've just done, we could stay at our current level of output and get rid of twenty-three or twenty-four staff. That's about $700,000 in salaries and costs saved. Not bad, eh?'

'But ...' said Julia.

'Not bad at all', said Johannson, cutting her off. 'I don't think we'll get any flak from the union; they've been pretty gutless in my last few run-ins with them. We'll sell it as a downsizing exercise — everybody's doing it — the lean, mean organisation, doing more with less — that kind of thing.'

'That's right — they'd just go to water if we present this as a fait accompli. And the shareholders should be pretty happy at the cost-saving', said Max. 'Jack, how could we re-do the layout if we had that fewer number of staff?'

'Well, let's see', said Tuttle, taking some plans from the shelf behind him and spreading them on the table. 'Now, these lads here — the volley-ball crowd that's always late back from lunch — they could go, and their machines could be shifted to ...'

As the conversation became more animated, Julia slumped in her chair, and wondered how things had got this far out of control.

Discuss roles, norms, cohesiveness and conformity in this group.

(Source: Reproduced with permission from Eunson (1990).)

MYTHS ABOUT TEAMWORK

by AMANDA SINCLAIR

Look at any of the popular strategies for boosting organisational performance and you will find that using teams is in there somewhere. Better-quality teamwork is seen as crucial to organisational effectiveness. But wishful thinking has jeopardised our capacity to create it. Aggressively marketed organisational solutions have overstated the healing properties and success rate of teams. The evidence about their effectiveness is nowhere near so clear-cut.

Of course, no-one wants to advertise the failures — the time and resources wasted in teams which are the vehicles for personal agendas, or where they deteriorate into exercises for avoiding accountability. Even worse are the teams that tyrannise their members and severely impair individual work capacity. They can have high fall-out costs in personal and bottom-line terms.

The most important requirement in making teams work is to abandon our illusions, to scrutinise and learn from past mistakes. Only by owning up will we be able to evaluate what teams do best and how. Only then will we have a good chance of designing and participating in teams that work.

There are five common illusions about teams.

Illusion 1: Teams can do anything

Lingering from the 1960s and 1970s, infatuation with human relations is the illusion that teams can do anything. The reality is that teams do some things very well and some things badly. Prospective team builders need to take a cold, hard look at what they really want a team to do. If it is to cover tracks, bury an issue under interminable meetings or give an appearance of consultation, then forget it.

Teams are not magic. They must have tasks that are achievable within a specified time frame. The team charged with 'management' has an impossible brief and will surely fail unless effort is spent spelling out what the management task involves and what constitutes success.

Neither are teams a cheap option. They inevitably consume resources and time. Teams rarely resolve conflict. More often, they pressure-cook it.

If an individual has the skills to do the job with the requisite creativity, then the individual, not the team, should do the job.

Teams should only be considered where there is a widely agreed case for their use. Teams are excellent devices for sharing skills and information creatively and they can coordinate big projects if the right people are team members.

Team tasks should also be relevant to present and future interests and skills of team members. If you want people to be committed to a team then it should have a personal career pay-off and not be seen as an onerous duty.

Illusion 2: Good teams are purely task-oriented

A second illusion is that good teams focus only on the task. Teams are there to get a job done. However, their existence as a group means that they have an emotional agenda as well as a task agenda. They have a life-cycle and momentum which determines when and under what circumstances the group will be likely to perform best and when it is vulnerable to diversion or disruption. The emotional agenda is as powerful, if not more so, in determining how well the group does its job. Teams need understanding of the emotional events that help and hinder performance, such as turnover of membership or lack of leadership.

They also need to experience achievement. An open-ended existence or indeterminate task can be offset by designing opportunities for feedback, ritual events and reporting schedules which enhance, not thwart, the team's momentum.

Illusion 3: Teams don't need leaders

A third illusion is that leaders are not necessary in good teams. Leadership is back in fashion. But people in teams often argue that good teamwork makes leadership redundant. Explicit or strong leadership behaviour is seen as contrary to the notional equality of teams.

This illusion and the lack of leadership it produces is one of the worst things that can happen to a team. It ensures an obsession with internal power relations and a team without a champion. A leader is the team's link with the wider organisation and the vital conduit for resources, support and credibility. Teams need help to understand how their leadership requirements change and how to make the most of the leadership resources distributed among members.

Illusion 4: Everyone belongs in a team

Another illusory belief is that everyone can find a place in a team. Team mythology has it that everyone can find a productive role and that, with enough skill building, people can play many different roles, depending upon what is required. This is to deny all the psychological evidence that many personality types do their best work alone.

As with sporting teams, no amounts of edicts from the coaches that 'you will be a team' will convert individualists into team players

Illusion 5: Teams are accountable

A final and controversial illusion is that teams can be held accountable. There is increasing attention to business ethics and the need to establish accountability for management actions. But how do you hold a team responsible? Teams are a time-honoured device for displacing responsibility and avoiding clear accountability. Bad decisions are put down to the members of the team who fall from favour.

Alternatively, if all the team members are to be held equally responsible, do you demand that they all resign or suffer penalties? This is hardly a practical solution, but it is frequently a political one.

Teams need to be designed with explicit recognition of where responsibility for their decisions and impacts lie. Teams have a better chance of being effective if they are a well-considered and well-resourced response to specific organisational requirements.

(Source: The *Weekend Australian*, April 7–8, 1990, p. 39. Reproduced with permission of the author.)

YOU DON'T SAY? More of what people say about groups and teams

If a committee is allowed to discuss a bad idea long enough, it will inevitably vote to implement the idea simply because so much work has already been done on it.

Ken Cruickshank

Individually, mediocrities do not add up to much. But the essence of mediocrities is that they do not act individually, nor are they individual-ists. They act collectively, in groups, where they have a lot of power — not power to create, facilitate, permit, to say 'yes', but power to destroy, obstruct, dilute, deny, to say 'no' — but power, for all that. Their use of this power, particularly against non-mediocre, individualistic individuals, is motivated by malice and envy, but also by the need for self-defence.
   This is the strongest power in the world.

Ian McEwan

Soloists are inspiring in opera and perhaps even in small entrepreneurial ventures, but there is no place for them in large corporations.

Norman R. Augustine,
President and CEO, Martin Marietta Corp.

Teamwork is consciously espoused but unwittingly shunned by most people in business because they are deathly afraid of it. They think it will render them anonymous, invisible.

Srully Blotnick,
management consultant

(Successful teambuilding) was as simple as realising that employees are adults who have responsibilities outside the workplace. We stopped telling people to check their brains at the front door in the morning and pick them up at five. We started treating people with respect.

Debra Boggan,
former plant manager, Northern Telecom, North Carolina

I don't like to work in a group. I don't get along well with other people.

Jimmy Breslin,
American journalist

Work teams and group leaders are a way of setting worker against worker.

Eddie Chapman,
union shop steward, Ford UK

United we stand, divided we fall.

Aesop's Fables

The ratio of We's to I's is the best indicator of the development of a team.

Lewis D. Eigen,
University Research Corp.

I was a dictator for eight years, but now that style doesn't work any more. For a time, I was afraid of losing my job. But then I thought that if I could make the transition from supervisor to coach, I would become an asset to the company ... I like work teams very much because it's like running my own business.

Rick Pederson,
Northern Telecom, North Carolina

... we can define team-building as an activity whereby members of a work-group (1) begin to understand more thoroughly the nature of group dynamics and effective teamwork, particularly the interrelationship of process and content, and (2) learn to apply certain principles and skills of group process towards greater team effectiveness.

W. Warner Burke

The team ideology tyrannises because, under the banner of benefits to all, teams are frequently used to camouflage coercion with the appearance of cohesion, conceal conflict with the appearance of consensus, convert conformity into an appearance of creativity, to give unilateral decisions a co-determinist seal of approval, to delay action in the supposed interests of consultation, to legitimate lack of leadership and to disguise expedient arguments and personal agendas.

Amanda Sinclair,
Melbourne University Graduate School of Management

The productivity of a work group seems to depend upon how the group members see their own goals in relation to the goals of the organisation.
Paul Hersey and Kenneth H. Blanchard

Intellectuals tend to be individualists, or even independents, are not team conscious and tend to regard obedience as a surrender of personality.
Harold Nicolson

It is most important that a (Japanese) meeting should reach a unanimous conclusion; it should leave no-one frustrated or dissatisfied, for this weakens ... unity and solidarity.

Chie Nakane

What the company wants is for us to work like the Japanese. Everybody go out and do jumping jacks in the morning and kiss each other when they go home at night. You work as a team, rat on each other, and lose control of your destiny. That's not going to work in (America).

John Brodie,
union official, United Paperworkers

Teamwork is essential. It allows you to blame someone else.
Finagle's Eighth Rule

LEADERSHIP AND EMPOWERMENT: THE DELICATE BALANCE

The exercise of leadership or authority or power is a very complex thing. Certainly it is true today to say that authority is quite different in most settings — organisations, the family, the community — than it was 100 years ago, or even twenty years ago. Within organisations, different styles of leadership are often apparent, and those styles can be understood in relation to the emphasis leaders place upon concern for the task — getting on with the job, and not bothering too much about human relationships — and concern for people — relating to personal needs, without worrying too much about the mechanics of administrative procedures. What is your leadership style? Complete the questionnaire in Exercise D and find out.

EXERCISE

D:
YOUR LEADERSHIP STYLE

Goal
To evaluate oneself in terms of the leadership dimensions of task orientation and people orientation.

Implementation
Without prior discussion, fill out the following leadership questionnaire.

Leadership questionnaire

Name: _____ **Group**: _____

Directions: The following items describe aspects of leadership behaviour. Respond to each item according to the way you would most likely act if you were the leader of a work group. Circle whether you would most likely behave in the described way: always (A), frequently (F), occasionally (O), seldom (S), or never (N).

	A	F	O	S	N
1. I would most likely act as the spokesperson of the group.					
2. I would encourage overtime work.					

	A	F	O	S	N
3. I would allow members complete freedom in their work.					
4. I would encourage the use of uniform procedures.					
5. I would permit the members to use their own judgement in solving problems.					
6. I would stress being ahead of competing groups.					
7. I would speak as a representative of the group.					
8. I would needle members for greater effort.					
9. I would try out my ideas in the group.					
10. I would let the members do their work the way they think best.					
11. I would be working hard for a promotion.					
12. I would tolerate postponement and uncertainty.					
13. I would speak for the group if there were visitors present.					
14. I would keep the work moving at a rapid pace.					
15. I would turn the members loose on a job and let them go to it.					
16. I would settle conflicts when they occur in the group.					
17. I would get swamped by details.					
18. I would represent the group at outside meetings.					
19. I would be reluctant to allow the members any freedom of action.					
20. I would decide what should be done and how it should be done.					
21. I would push for increased production.					
22. I would let some members have authority which I could keep.					

(continued)

	A	F	O	S	N
23. Things would usually turn out as I had predicted.					
24. I would allow the group a high degree of initiative.					
25. I would assign group members to particular tasks.					
26. I would be willing to make changes.					
27. I would ask the members to work harder.					
28. I would trust the group members to exercise good judgement.					
29. I would schedule the work to be done.					
30. I would refuse to explain my actions.					
31. I would persuade others that my ideas are to their advantage.					
32. I would permit the group to set its own pace.					
33. I would urge the group to beat its previous record.					
34. I would act without consulting the group.					
35. I would ask that group members follow standard rules and regulations.					

T _____   P _____

(Source: Adapted from Sergiovanni, Metzcus, and Burden's revision of the Leadership Behaviour Description Questionnaire, *American Educational Research Journal*, 6 (1969), pp 62–79. Reproduced with permission.)

Scoring

1. In order to locate yourself on the Leadership Profile Sheet, you will score your own questionnaire on the dimensions of task orientation (T) and people orientation (P).
2. The scoring is as follows:
    (a) Circle the item number for items 8, 12, 17, 18, 19, 30, 34, and 35.
    (b) Write the number 1 in front of a *circled item number* if you responded seldom (S) or N (never) to that item.
    (c) Also write a number 1 in front of *item numbers not circled* if you responded A (always) or F (frequently).
    (d) Circle the number 1s which you have written in front of the following items: 3, 5, 8, 10, 15, 18, 19, 22, 24, 26, 28, 30, 32, 34, and 35.

(e) Count the circled number 1s. This is your score for the level of your concern for people. Record the score in the blank following the letter P at the end of the questionnaire.

(f) Count the uncircled number 1s. This is your score for your concern for the task. Record this number in the blank following the letter T.

3. Next, look at the Leadership Style Profile sheet below and follow the directions.

Variations

1. Participants can predict how they will appear on the profile prior to scoring the questionnaire.

2. Paired participants already acquainted can predict each other's scores. If they are not acquainted, they can discuss their reactions to the questionnaire items to find some bases for this prediction.

3. The leadership styles represented on the profile sheet can be illustrated through role playing. A relevant situation can be set up, and the 'leaders' can be coached to demonstrate the styles being studied.

4. Subgroups can be formed of participants similarly situated on the shared leadership scale. These groups can be assigned identical tasks to perform. The work generated can be processed in terms of morale and productivity.

Leadership style profile sheet

Name: _____ **Group**: _____

Directions: To determine your style of leadership, mark your score on the concern for task dimension (T) on the left-hand arrow in figure 3.1. Next, move to the right-hand arrow and mark your score on the concern for people dimension (P). Draw a straight line that intersects the P and T scores. The point at which that line crosses the shared leadership arrow indicates your score on that dimension.

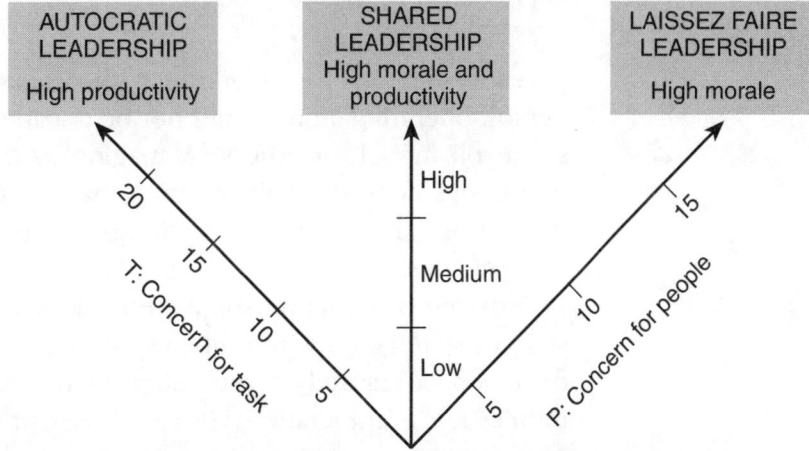

Figure 3.1: T-P Leadership Model

(Source: 'T-P Leadership Questionnaire: An Assessment of Style', from Pfeiffer, J. William and Jones, John E. (eds.) *A Handbook of Structured Experiences for Human Relations Training*, Vol. 1, pp 7–8, 10–12.)

GROUPS, TEAMS AND LEADERSHIP

Groups need leaders, but do teams? The British Special Air Service, or SAS, was designed around four-man combat teams, in contrast to the traditional eight or ten men led by a non-commissioned officer. The number four was chosen to prevent orthodox leadership behaviour from emerging, so that a 'unique military democracy' could emerge, with all four members deferring to the specialised expertise of each other but combining specialised and general skills to produce a highly synergistic style of operating. Yet, when the teams return from field operations, they integrate back into a traditional, hierarchical set-up with clear lines between leaders and led. Alvin Toffler sees this oscillation between two modes of functioning — from hierarchical to nonhierarchical command, and then back again, as needs demand — as a model for future organisations.[1] Can organisations really be this flexible? And if it is possible to dispense with leadership in some situations, might it not be possible to dispense with it in many or all situations? With the proliferation of teams in organisations, are leaders becoming an endangered species?

What is it that leaders do anyway? The tasks or roles of a leader can be summed up with the nonsense acronym SPORTMoB/CaDaCaDaCa.

S	Staffing
P	Planning
O	Organising
R	Reporting
T	Training
Mo	Motivating
B	Budgeting
C	Communicating
D	Directing
C	Coordinating
D	Delegating
C	Counselling

Leadership involves working with others to get things done. Thus a person operating alone could not be a leader (except if that person was, say, a role-model for others). Managing, as the old definition goes, is getting things done through others. A manager/leader does this by ordering the led or subordinates to do things, or else by delegating to the led or subordinates.

Ordering or directing someone to do something implies an autocratic style of leadership, where no responsibility or independence of thought or action is granted to the subordinate. Delegating a task to someone implies a less autocratic style: to a lesser or greater extent, responsibility or independence of thought and action is granted to the subordinates.

It is an ancient maxim of management technique that responsibility should be matched by an equal degree of power or authority. If someone is delegated a task, but insufficient power to do it, then that person is set up for failure.

Concern with the power to get things done, together with the rise of teams in organisations, has led some people to prefer the word *empowerment* rather than delegation, because, to their ears, it has more of a positive, action-oriented sound.[2]

Many of the things that managers traditionally did can now be done by teams (in fact, some would say that this has always been the case). As teams are empowered to do more of the tasks such as planning, reporting, organising, coordinating, budgeting, communicating and even staffing, the directing function becomes problematic and the role of the manager or supervisor shrivels up to, or expands to (depending upon your point of view) motivating, training, counselling and delegating. Increasingly, the role of a manager or supervisor is being seen not as a controller but as a coach, a facilitator, a 'sponsor', someone who is not so much hands-on as hands-off in style.[3]

This, to say the least, is quite threatening for many managers and supervisors. It basically entails a substantial transfer in power or control from traditional holders to non-traditional holders, i.e., team members.

Rollin Glaser has devised a model of this transfer with his Facilitative Leadership Model[4] (figure 3.2). Such a transition involves the learning of many new behaviours, the unlearning of many old ones and the invasion of many people's territories, and thus it is unwise to expect substantial changes in a workplace for at least a year, and probably longer.

Glaser argues that the leader shifts role from that of a controller to that of a facilitator or coach — someone who facilitates or sets up the pre-conditions for change and action rather than initiates change and action. Instead of making things happen, the leader now makes things happen so that others can make things happen. In Glaser's view, the leader thus doesn't lose, but gains power — to the extent that the leader empowers others, to that same extent he or she empowers him, or herself, and is, in fact, a superleader. This is because if power is the ability to get things done, then empowerment, or delegation of others, means that the collective output of the leader, or facilitator, and the team goes up in comparison to the level that prevailed under traditional power relationships.

This poses some vexed questions about power: Is it divisible? Can giving it away make it come back, and in a strengthened form? Advocates of teams would say 'yes' to both questions; critics of teams would say 'no' to both questions.

Let's go further on this, and ask: 'What is power?' How do you define it? A useful way of looking at power is to look at five bases of power, namely legitimate power, reward power, coercive power, referent power and expert power.

Legitimate power is the power that comes from being in an authoritative position. This is the power wielded by village elders, police officers, military officers and elected officials, but it is also present in organisations, where the boss is the boss *because* she is the boss. The more hierarchical is the organisation, the more overt will be the legitimate power wielded by the boss.

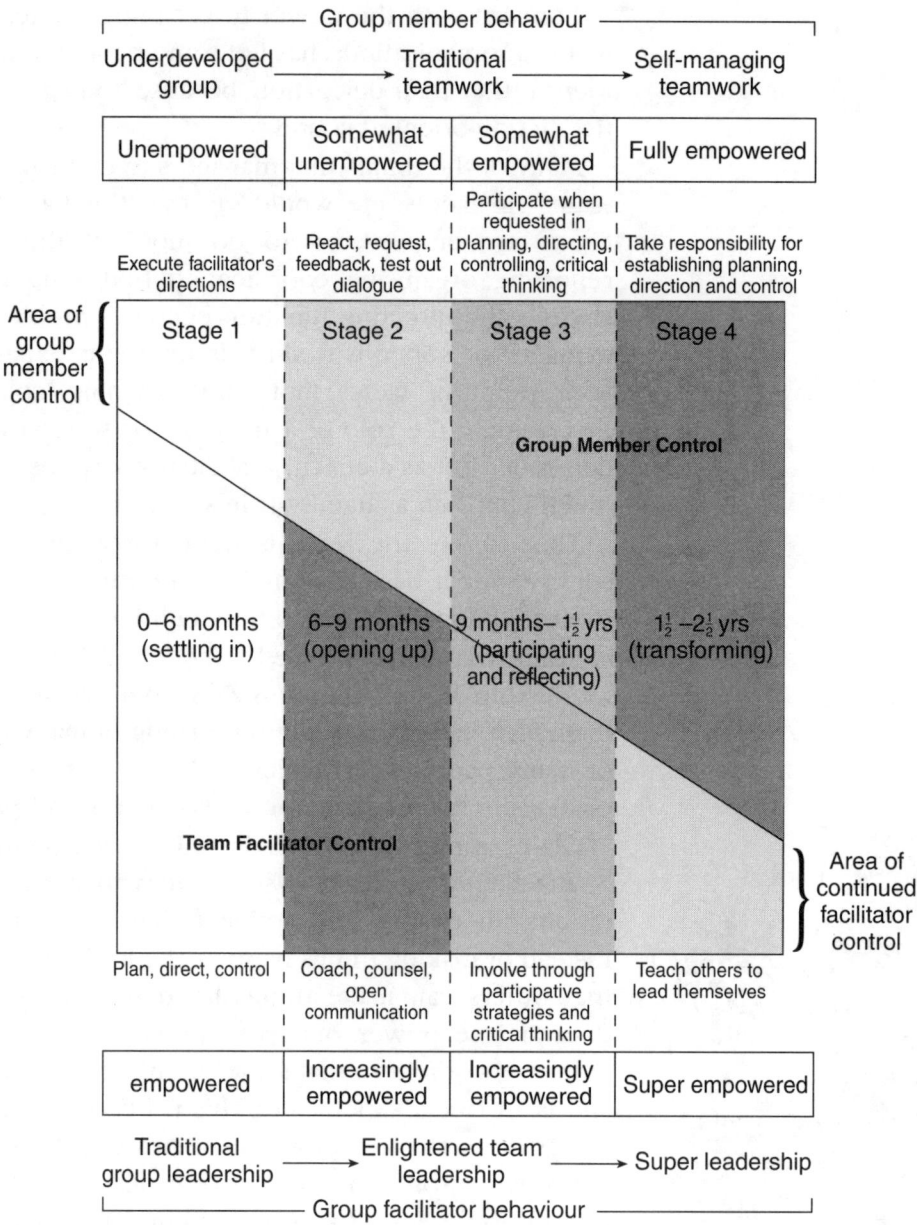

	Group member behaviour		
Underdeveloped group	→ Traditional teamwork	→ Self-managing teamwork	

Unempowered	Somewhat unempowered	Somewhat empowered	Fully empowered
Execute facilitator's directions	React, request, feedback, test out dialogue	Participate when requested in planning, directing, controlling, critical thinking	Take responsibility for establishing planning, direction and control

Area of group member control

Stage 1	Stage 2	Stage 3	Stage 4

Group Member Control

0–6 months (settling in)	6–9 months (opening up)	9 months–$1\frac{1}{2}$ yrs (participating and reflecting)	$1\frac{1}{2}$–$2\frac{1}{2}$ yrs (transforming)

Team Facilitator Control

Area of continued facilitator control

Plan, direct, control	Coach, counsel, open communication	Involve through participative strategies and critical thinking	Teach others to lead themselves

empowered	Increasingly empowered	Increasingly empowered	Super empowered

Traditional group leadership	→ Enlightened team leadership	→ Super leadership	

| | Group facilitator behaviour | | |

Figure 3.2: Facilitative Leadership Model

(Source: Glaser, 1992: 9, reproduced with the permission of Organisation Design and Development, Inc., King of Prussia, PA.)

Reward power is fairly self-evident. A person has reward power if he is able to grant pay increases or improvements in conditions, give more responsibility, and assign more interesting work. The other side of this coin is coercive power.

Coercive power exists when a person is able to punish or to instil fear, by means of dismissal, demotion or by cutting salary or forcing a transfer, or recommending that one of these outcomes occurs.

Referent power flows from the intrinsic qualities of an individual. The wielder of referent power may have 'charisma', or may simply be so stylish, handsome or possess other personal characteristics that people wish to emulate them. A typical instance of referent power is when a sports or movie star endorses a product (which as often as not has nothing to do with sport or acting).

Expert power is wielded by people who seem to have access to special information, skill, experience or training. Even though societies, particularly societies with strong anti-intellectual values, sometimes denigrate the value of 'expert opinion', within organisations it is unwise to ignore the opinions of the tax specialist, the lawyer, the personnel manager, the data-processing whiz and the assembly-line hot shot.

Generally speaking, the story of power bases in organisations — and society at large, for that matter — in the past thirty or so years has been the decline of legitimate power and the rise of expert power. Reward power and coercive power — the carrot and the stick — have waxed and waned according to economic circumstances (Is it a catastrophe if I lose my job? Will a small raise in pay motivate me to try harder?) and organisational structuring (Are rewards and punishments the domain of my immediate boss — for example, via appraisal systems — or are they the domain of the human resources department, operating within a wider industrial relations context?). Referent power is difficult to pin down in organisations, but there does not appear to have been a systematic rise or decline in it.

People these days tend to be less accepting of authority for its own sake: they want a reason, not an order. This partial rejection of authority seems to be linked with the rise in educational levels of people entering the workforce. The power gap between leaders and led has sometimes shrunk as society and organisations have become more technologically-based. The more complex the technology, the greater is the power of those who understand that technology — in extremity, if they withdraw their labour, the whole show collapses. On the other hand, to the extent that automation and expert computer systems take the place of human labour, then the expert power base of technical specialists declines. Thus, as legitimate power bases have declined, expert power bases have become more dominant — a dominance modified by legitimate power wielders having access to the expert power of inanimate sytems.

Expert power and shared leadership in teams

Society has not only become more technologically-based, it has become much more complex. There is an information explosion occurring out there, and it's getting bigger and louder all the time. This simply means that it is becoming harder and harder for an individual to know all there is to know about one field, let alone that field and the surrounding fields that provide a context of causes and effects. This means that within society generally, and organisations specifically, there are strong forces impelling us to move away from individual decision-making to group-based decision-making.

But who leads such groups or teams? What power bases do such leaders draw upon? Expert power appears to be becoming the dominant power base, but can one person be an expert in all areas with which a team deals? Almost certainly no. To a certain extent, a leader may abdicate the role of being an expert or specialist and concentrate upon being a generalist — someone able to communicate with specialists from differing fields and able to facilitate communication among those specialists. To that extent, a generalist is, in fact, a communications or process specialist.

Another solution may be to pursue shared or distributed leadership, which simply means that whoever has expertise in a particular field — data processing, wiring up the number six machine, resolving conflict and producing consensus in meetings — is the leader of the team for that particular phase of operations.[5] There also has to be a high degree of trust within the team that the presiding expert really is expert, and not a victim of 'educated incapacity' blind spots, and also that the expert is not baffling the rest with a wall of jargon with a view to building their own empire.

Such shared leadership, however, may be easier described than realised. Critics of teams and shared leadership point out that it is difficult to ascribe accountability to a team, whereas it is quite simple to make an individual leader accountable.[6] What do you do if a team performs disastrously? Do you fire the whole team? For that matter, who gets rewarded if the team performs at a very high level? Is it everyone on the team, irrespective of differences in individual contributions to output?[7] A pressing problem in traditional organisations has been that delegation often fails because not enough power is given to match responsibility. The problems that arise with teams seem to concern the opposite notion: does empowerment sometimes fail because of 'the harlot's prerogative'[8] — not enough responsibility is taken to match the power given?

There is a tension, therefore, between the idea of teams and the idea of leadership. Are leaders obsolete? Is everyone a leader? Or is leadership still the preserve of a few, who, through talent, drive or luck or a mixture of these, exert a sway over the many? What happens if a leader, or a non-leader individual with expertise, is simply more competent than a team? And what if leaders are reluctant — as they have been throughout history — to give up power?

QUESTIONS, QUESTIONS ...

1. How might teams be made more accountable?
2. Can we do without leaders altogether?
3. Consider three leaders you know. What mixture of power bases (legitimate, reward, coercive, referent, expert) do they have?
4. What are the limitations of expert power and shared leadership?

THE INTERNAL POLITICS OF TEAMS

by ROSABETH MOSS KANTER

Origins of team politics

Of course, declaring people a 'team' does not automatically make them one, nor does seeking decisions in which many people have a voice ensure that democratic procedures will prevail. A philosophy of participation in no way eliminates jockeying for status or internal competition if people bring self-serving interests into a group, or if they have differential stakes in the outcome, or if they come from segmented organisations whose structure and culture encourages divisiveness and non-cooperation across areas. There may be differential advantages to individual members to be gained by pushing particular decisions over others; there may be differential benefits to be reaped outside the group by appearing to be a dominant force in it — like the ambitious young manager who wants to impress his boss with his 'leadership' skills. People bring different needs and interests into any kind of group from their location outside it, and these can serve as the origins of team politics.

Team members: insiders or outsiders?

How much differential needs and interests politicise a team is in large measure a function of how the team is set up in the first place. Group dynamics become more competition-centred when rewards or recognition outside the team are scarce, and members are direct competitors for them. There is also more internal politicking when some functions, represented by team members, think they stand to lose by certain decisions of the team, and the representing member is under pressure from colleagues as well as personally concerned. It is a simple psychic-economic calculation: do the gains from dropping certain interests/goals in the name of cooperation outweigh the losses? Cooperation and reduced politicking are more likely to occur when team members are participating in the group as individuals rather than as representatives, because they can make individual deals free of the pressure of a 'shadow group' symbolically looking over their shoulders. (Indeed, when teams begin to jell as cooperative entities, even representatives sometimes forget their external group affiliation in favour of team identification — sometimes to the detriment of the constituency supposedly being served by the participation of its representative.)

Teams that tyrannise

Beyond the politics of interest maximisation, teams are also arenas for the flexing of power muscles in and of themselves. There is often nothing inherently more 'democratic' about certain decisions because they were made by teams rather than by individual managers. Teams can turn into oligarchies, with a few dominant people taking over and forcing the others to fall into line. There are many examples of supposedly representative mechanisms sliding into oligarchies — e.g., the reputed takeover of some unions by small groups with shady ties. The benign 'tyranny' of peers can substitute for the benign 'tyranny' of managers, with conformity pressures as strong and sanctions for deviance as impelling. In one highly participative factory, workers complained that they felt too dependent on their teams for evaluation and job security and feared being ostracised by a clique. Members of autonomous work teams in a Cummins Engine plant were likely to be harder on absent members, according to a former plant manager, than management would have dared to be; they would often appear at the doorstep to drag a person in to work if the claimed illness did not satisfy members. (of course, they relied on each other's contributions more than in a conventional work situation.) Indeed, management often counts on this peer pressure to stay in line as a side benefit of participation.

Some teams prefer to fall divided than stand united

Finally, teams become politicised when there are historic tensions between members that have not been resolved before the 'team' is formed, tensions that are more likely in category-conscious, segmentalist cultures than in integrative ones, where ties cut across levels, functions and social categories.

These tensions can rise to greater importance when hostile parties are thrown together and forced to interact, especially if they have to rely on each other for reasonable outcomes. This statement challenges a classic social-psychological cliché, based on a famous experiment by Muzafer and Carolyn Sherif, that groups in conflict who suddenly find themselves dependent on each other for survival develop 'superordinate goals' which relieve the tensions; they discovered this by fostering group rivalry and then imposing a crisis at a summer camp. But that was summer camp, not a corporation. Experience from joint labour-management participation in problem-solving suggests that there are circumstances in which hostility may increase, not decrease. If no attempt has been made to create a more integrative system, to resolve tensions and improve communication before the meeting, and if the situation is frustrating — as meetings can easily be — the emotions may rise to the surface, and members of the opposing camps may start blaming each other for team problems. At British Rail, participation by worker representatives in management

(continued)

meetings resulted in increased tension between managers and workers, especially because worker representatives tended to include those more critical of management.

The myth of 'team'

'Inequality' and 'politics' in team discussions are not generically so bad. After all, the people we are talking about have learned to live with both in the rest of their service in the corporate hierarchy. Dominance of the 'best' — most skilled, most informed — participators seems likely to produce better decisions. 'Political' discussions may mean that a variety of interests are more accurately reflected in ultimate decisions. So the solution to the problems of lowered commitment that these phenomena create should not lie in expecting the skilled and informed to stay out of discussions or those with special needs or interests to forget them. But that 'solution' — holding back — is in fact what is fostered by the next dilemma of participation, 'team' mythology.

The mythology that surrounds the idea of a 'team' in many organisations holds that differences among members do not exist — because they are now a 'team' — and therefore it is not legitimate to acknowledge them or talk about them. Everyone has to act as if they were all sharing equally in the operations of the group. While inside the team, they have to pretend that they do not see that some are more able than others, or that the highest-level people are dominating, or that the chair is railroading another decision through. Where 'team' mythology is strong, only an outsider — a consultant or facilitator or naive outsider — can open it for examination.

(Source: *The Change Masters: Innovations for Productivity in the American Corporation* (New York: Simon and Schuster, 1983, pp. 260–262). Reproduced with permission.)

INFORMATION SCANNING

THE BASIS OF COMMUNICATION

GETTING THE DATA FOR TEAMS

We have now considered the group dynamics and power factors in teams. Once the teams in which we operate can begin to manage these factors, we can consider the various communication skills and processes that are needed to make a team truly effective.

If you look again at the model of communication in teams (p. 2), you will see that before teams and their members can begin to develop skills such as giving feedback, listening and seeking consensus, they need to have inputs of basic information.

These inputs are not the result of some neutral, technocratic process involving inanimate systems such as computers, or certainly not only that. The first prerequisite is that an empowered workforce has access to the data it needs to do the job, and as we have seen, in many workplaces self-managing teams have access to information about production, budgets, staffing and other areas that were traditionally the preserve of managers only. There has to be a climate of trust for information-sharing, not a climate of fear: as W. Edwards Deming, one of the pioneers of the industrial quality movement, has put it: 'A fearful workplace creates bad data.'[1]

Team staff may also need training in quality control techniques so that they can gather data, and then manipulate and interpret it. Team members who are 'boundary spanners' operate within the team and outside it — talking to other teams, senior management, other areas (production, marketing, design, personnel), and customers — and then bring that information back into the team. Team members may be able to do a lot of reality checking by plugging into the grapevines, or the rumour mills, that operate both inside and outside the organisation.

Team members have to be able to ask questions, and ask the right questions. They have to be able to research and learn. They have to bring the data back to the team, building data bases and sharing information with other team members.

Once the information is fed back into the team, productivity can often rise. Video monitors and display boards showing output targets against previous best performances can motivate people to try harder, as compared to workplaces where teams or individuals have no data against which to measure their performance. Teams can amaze managements with their thirst for more information: teams in a priority-package delivery organisation saw that gainsharing — profit sharing — gave them a specific incentive to be more productive, and thus their information-seeking and communication behaviour with management and among themselves increased substantially — as did their productivity.[2]

QUESTIONS, QUESTIONS ...

1. Think of a task or series of tasks you perform within an organisation. Is there a gap between the information you have and the information you would like to have about that task or those tasks?
2. What feedback do you have on your own performance of tasks?

5

PERCEIVING AND EXPRESSING
COMMUNICATION SKILLS

NON-VERBAL COMMUNICATION IN TEAMS

We need to know the silent language of non-verbal communication if we are to understand what is going on in teams. Looks, gestures, posture, eye contact, the intonation of words, even the very environment in which we find ourselves — all of these factors are as important as the words we speak, and sometimes even more important. Consider, for example, the section on roles (p. 27) — the non-verbal behaviour of the different role types gives us critical insights into the total behavioural picture. As two observers of group processes, Ernest Stech and Sharon Ratliffe, put it:

(Remember this) basic communication principle: the meaning is not in the message; the meaning is in the persons who are communicating ... Every message has two levels: content and relationship. The content level consists of what is actually said and is made up primarily of the verbal code ... the relationship level of a message often is established more by how *a statement is made (non-verbal cues) than by* what *is said (verbal cues). What we say and how we say it affects other people and their feelings. It indicates who has power and who does not. It establishes who will team up with whom. It creates and defines the way people treat each other. This is an absolutely vital point. You cannot understand what is going on in a group meeting without knowing about the relationships between members. Who likes whom? Who cannot get along with whom? Who is considered competent? Who is seen as caring and considerate? Who belongs to cliques or coalitions? These factors often have a far greater bearing on the outcome of a group meeting than the more rational matters of information and deduction and decision-making.*[1]

The silent language can be seen in numerous ways in teams. When people are talking together, for example, the change in roles of listeners and speakers is regulated by a subtle dance of eye contact and voice intonation: when a person is talking, he or she may break continuous eye contact with others while speaking, re-establishing gaze only when ready to 'yield the floor' to other persons. This is usually accompanied by a drop in voice intonation to cue the changeover in an implicit way, or a rise in intonation, as in a question, to cue a response in an explicit way.[2] If a person keeps on talking, while avoiding eye contact and keeping to the same intonation, it is very difficult for others to take over the speaker role, try as they might to emit all the standard 'bidding' signals — raising a finger or hand or pen, raising eyebrows, nodding the head, wetting or smacking of lips, sitting more alertly, moving the body, making progressively louder and more rapid 'friendly grunts' ('Mm-mm', 'Uh-huh'). These cues are obviously visual, and therefore may be missed by people who are looking elsewhere, or who are blind or visually handicapped.[3]

Teams thrive on members showing behaviours of alertness and empathy, rather than, say, behaviours of boredom or hostility. Boredom can be seen in glazed expressions, slumped posture, continual looking at the wall clock or watches, prolonged doodling, yawning ('a yawn is a silent scream'), drumming of fingers, tapping of pens, jiggling of legs, winking and averting eye contact. Hostility or disapproval doesn't have to be overt; it can be conveyed via shaking of heads, pursing of lips, tapping of pens, picking imaginary lint off clothes, doodling violently, rolling of eyes, conspiratorial winking, facial expressions of despair, sighing, non-attendance.

Empathy, or being of a like mind, can also be seen in spatial orientation, and postural and gestural behaviour. People who are well-acquainted tend to sit closer together and tolerate crowding more easily; the same holds true of females as compared to males, and people of the same age and social status as compared to people of differing ages and status.

Similarly, people making collective judgements tend to sit closer together than they do when they are making individual judgements. Empathy can also be shown by turning and leaning towards people we like (and turning and leaning away from those we don't like). It is also shown by echoing or mirroring other people's postures and gestures. We do this because we like the other person we are (unconsciously) imitating, or else because we are impressed by their higher status.[4]

The same behaviour can express different emotions — it all depends on the context. Non-verbal behaviour can also be at odds with verbal behaviour. Thus a team member may say, 'It looks okay to me', while scratching her head, shaking her head, sighing, and scoring broad pen-strokes through the agenda papers. Which message do you believe? Which channel is carrying the true feeling? In such situations, there is non-verbal 'leakage', or the verbal and non-verbal messages are not congruent. It is probably wiser to 'listen' to the non-verbal message here, and infer that the member doesn't think that it's okay. It's also wise not to just leave things at that point — non-verbal communication can be ambiguous and confusing. Follow up verbally, and ask the member if she perhaps has reservations.

Non-verbal communication is also the channel via which status is often displayed. Status displays are key symbols of hierarchical inequality, and can kill off, or at least weaken, any team spirit. Thus for example, in a hierarchical organisation such as the US Navy, an admiral found that he got most out of his team when he adjourned formal proceedings, went to another room, took off his uniform coat and smoked a cigar. The shift from the formal to the informal context, from hierarchical to non-hierarchical role, was the catalyst for a more frank exchange of views.[5]

High status, or at least the self-perception of high status, is also indicated by other signals such as staking out a larger than average amount of territory at a table (by spreading out briefcase, books, coffee cup, etc.), suddenly getting close to another person, a penetrating stare, loud voice, patronisingly patting others, adopting a relaxed posture when others are more alert, and looking up when talking, paying little attention to others (a power demonstration, indicating that the speaker does not feel the need to establish eye contact with others to check to see if they are accepting what is being said). High status or dominant individuals will often sit in a central position, such as at the head of a rectangular table, or across from as many others as possible. Others may choose to sit away from them (someone arriving late may experience stress, or at least discomfort, if forced to sit next to a high-status person, such as a leader or chairman). Equal spatial distribution of people around a table may imply a perceived equality among participants, and thus there will be a fair amount of conversation across the table, with few side conversations. When a group has a dominating leader, however, there tend to be more side conversations.[6]

Non-verbal messages can also be conveyed by our environment, and how we choose to structure that environment sends out powerful messages about territorial and status behaviour. It is considered that team effectiveness tends to be maximised by shared open-plan work layouts with few status symbols on display:

> *Often the mere layout of desks or workstations inhibits free communication. Ask how necessary separate offices/workrooms really are and whether they are acting as barriers to communications. Territorial barriers are barriers to communication.*
>
> Mike Woodcock[7]

> *Workplace equity and work-force trust are enhanced when perks and status symbols and, most important, true power distributions between organisational levels are reduced. Perks reward — they also distract and punish. Oriental rugs, private parking, corner offices, mahogany desks, even office sizes based on rank are destructive because they focus everyone's efforts on securing the trappings of status rather than teamwork.*
>
> D. Keith Denton[8]

Several obvious signs of hierarchical inequality also doom any team-building effort. Reserved parking spaces, privileged office locations, and many other signs of status may reinforce the efforts of the few, but they undermine the morale of the many who are denied. Most companies that work at day-to-day team-building downplay or eliminate such unpopular signals that say that some are more equal than others.

Paul S. George[9]

In ineffective groups or teams, words tend to be the province of thoughts, and non-verbal communication tends to be the province of feelings. Also, and partly because of this phenomenon, there tends to be a lack of congruence between the verbal and the non-verbal.

With effective teams, the opposite is the case: verbal and non-verbal behaviour are congruent, and words are used to openly express feelings as well as thoughts. Let's now consider feelings and emotions in greater detail.

EMOTION AND OPINION: KEY TOOLS OF COMMUNICATION

So much communication within groups and teams occurs at the socio-emotional level rather than the task level. This is the world of feelings, opinions, trust, lack of trust, empathy, sympathy, antipathy, and other fuzzy, difficult-to-measure qualities.

This makes many of us uncomfortable: many of us think — or is it feel? — that emotions have no place in public settings, that emotions are part of our private world, and to the extent that they are unleashed in the public world, then to that same extent they trigger unmanageable conflict.

This attitude ignores several important but uncomfortable truths:
- conflict is normal, not abnormal
- conflict can be unhealthy, but it can also be healthy
- your emotions go with you, wherever you go
- opinions can be more important than facts.[10]

A team member might say: 'Let's remain calm and rational here — let's stick to facts.' This might be a very useful approach when the team is about to explode with conflicting emotions and opinions, but it might be less than useful for the majority of encounters of team members. In fact, if team members continually suppress emotions and opinions at lower levels of conflict, then there is a very good chance that this bottling up will lead to a dramatic uncorking and eruption — usually at the most inconvenient and damaging of times.

Management theorist Peter Drucker has observed that one should not get the facts first, but instead get opinions first, then the facts.[11] His reasoning behind this is that facts can be recruited to serve any point of view; it is very rarely that 'the facts speak for themselves.' Because of this it makes sense to get people's opinions, prejudices and values out in the open as soon as possible. If this is not done, then selfish interests and hidden agendas may operate to ensure that one, rather than another, conclusion flows from a body of facts.

We like to think that we are disinterested seekers after truth and problem-solving, but not only is this rarely the case, it may not even be such a good thing: as Oscar Wilde remarked:

It is only about things that do not interest one that one can give a really unbiased opinion, which is no doubt the reason why an unbiased opinion is absolutely valueless.[12]

It is important, then, to get our opinions out in the open, and it may be even more important to get our *feelings* out into the open. Psychologist Bob Montgomery advises members of work teams to express feelings first when trying to solve problems. This is not because rationality is not important — it is — nor is it because work groups should try to re-create the high emotional intensity of encounter groups. Rather, it is because when we try to keep our feelings to ourselves, it compels others to try and read our minds. However, the more strain there is in a situation or relationship — the higher the level of latent or actual conflict — the more likely it is that any mind-reading will be wrong. Montgomery suggests that the choice we face in dealing with others is not:

Will I share my feelings with others?

but rather:

Will I share my feelings accurately, or will I make other people read my mind, knowing they will probably get it wrong just when it would be helpful if they got it right?[13]

The problem with not levelling with your feelings then is that people might get you wrong. But there's an equally good chance that they will get you right, try as you might to conceal your feelings: the reason for this is it is extremely difficult for you to totally control your body language, or non-verbal communication, and your true feelings are often expressed through this channel. Non-verbal 'leakage', or lack of congruence between your verbal and non-verbal communication, can give others quite a clear picture of what you think you are concealing.

Gene Bocialetti points out that emotions are nowhere more present, potent, but also manageable, than in the context of work teams, because: 'Work teams typically provide enough diversity — in member viewpoints and representation — and enough immediate contact through many face-to-face encounters to generate much emotion.'[14]

Groups or teams have formal and informal norms, as we saw earlier. Psychologist Irving Janis found[15] that the group advising President John F. Kennedy at the time of the Cuban Bay of Pigs invasion fiasco in 1961 was dominated by a norm of suppressing some emotions and unwisely yielding to others — suppression of personal doubts for fear of appearing 'soft', avoidance of conflict, intimidation by Robert F. Kennedy, the president's charisma, and his advisors' need to be liked by the president (see Groupthink, p. 42).

Bocialetti believes that the experience of the Kennedy group is fairly typical in most organisations, where the norm also is that of suppressing emotions. Such a norm is reinforced by frequent utterances such as: 'Let's be objective here' and 'I don't think there's any need for emotional outbursts.' When we think of emotions in work groups, we all too often only think of negative ones — hatred, depression, frustration, rejection, boredom — but we should also be thinking of positive ones — excitement, hope, gratitude, love, inspiration. If emotions, both positive and negative, are continually suppressed, however, the negative consequences outweigh the apparent benefits of 'unemotional' decision-making[16] (see table 5.1).

Table 5.1: Causes and effects of people suppressing their emotions in teams

NEGATIVE EMOTIONS	
Apparent undesirable effects of expressing negative emotions	**What happens when people suppress negative emotions**
• intimidating and frightening others • embarrassment, becoming the focus of attention • overstating one's views • provoking defensive or hostile responses • reflecting self-absorption, overconcern with oneself • loss of control of oneself • distracting others from 'real' work • disruption or termination of relationships	• internal body and psychological stress • withdrawal from participation • loss of energy, and depression (when anger is directed inward) • reduction of learning (e.g., Bay of Pigs situation) • important data for work is hidden • problems (and emotions) fester, often affecting implementation • opportunities to influence others are lost (messages carrying clear, responsible and appropriate emotional 'loading' are memorable and are more likely to be influential)
POSITIVE EMOTIONS	
Apparent undesirable effects of expressing positive emotions	**What happens when people suppress positive emotions**
• looking silly and awkward • being uncomfortable and violating norms • appearing naive • feeling too close too quickly • becoming the butt of jokes (e.g., 'Why don't you two kiss?') • appearing 'unbusinesslike' • appearing seductive (a problem in both heterogeneous groups and homogeneous groups)	• keeping others from being affirmed and recognised • dampening motivation • weakening the basis for receiving critical or negative affect or feedback • causing one to lose influence, as people tend to be more open to influence in an environment that is explicitly affirming

(Source: Adapted with permission from NTL Institute, 'Teams and the Management of Emotions', by Gene Bocialetti, pp. 65–66, *Team Building: Blueprints for Productivity and Satisfaction*, edited by W. Brendan Reddy with Kaleel Jamison, © 1988.)

FINDING OUT ABOUT OURSELVES AND OTHERS: THE JOHARI WINDOW

Non-verbal leakage implies that there is a lot about our emotions of which we are not aware. This is also obvious when we get caught in a communication breakdown: someone gets excited or upset, and we are left wondering what happened. Was it my fault? What did I say? What did I do?

If much of our own behaviour appears unable to be known, surely this also applies to others — they must be similarly unaware of much of their own behaviour. How do we find out more about ourselves, to know ourselves better? How do we let others know what we know about them?

A useful tool for finding out about ourselves is the Johari Window, originally devised by Joseph Luft and Harry Ingham (Johari = JOseph + HAR(ry)I).[17] The Johari Window has four panes (figure 5.1), but these panes can be of different sizes.

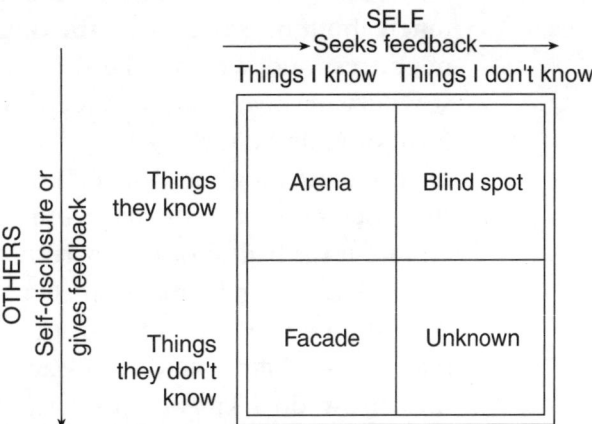

Figure 5.1: The Johari Window

The first area is the *Arena*, which is the area which is known to ourselves and also known to others. This is public domain in this pane: we have control over information and behaviour here, and we are comfortable with others knowing about such information and behaviour. These might be names, appearance, marital status, long-held and publicly aired opinions, mannerisms of which we are aware, and so on.

The second area is the *Blind Spot*: in here we find information and behaviour of which we are not currently aware, but others are. On the down side, this might comprise factors such as bad breath, and also displaying — via slips of the tongue and body language — dislike of people whom we think we like, while on the upside, it might be our being not-so-blissfully unaware that other people really like us.

The third area is called the *Facade*: here, we find information and behaviour of which we are aware, but which we choose not to reveal to others. Here live our dark secrets, but also more innocuous facts, opinions and behaviour that we simply decide to suppress at certain times when dealing with certain people, but which we bring into the Arena area at other times and when dealing with other people.

Finally, we have the *Unknown* area: this is unknown to others, and also unknown to ourselves, and comprises information and behaviour which lies within our subconscious mind. Material within this pane may never move to the other panes at all, or else it may emerge when changed circumstances call forth hitherto unsuspected motives, feelings, opinions and behaviour.

Feedback and self-disclosure

The relative sizes of Arena, Blind Spot and Facade — and to a lesser extent, Unknown — are determined by the way we interact with others. Our Blind Spot can be made smaller, for example, by others giving feedback — observations, opinions — to us, but the extent to which others give us feedback usually is strongly influenced by the extent to which we send out signals, vibes, that we are ready to listen to others — that we actively seek or solicit feedback. If others perceive us to be prickly and defensive, as someone who not only doesn't want to hear good or bad news but in fact is ready to shoot the messenger, then we won't hear much about ourselves from the outside world. 'And a good thing, too', you might respond. Why should the opinions of others worry you? Well, they should worry you because feedback from others is the most important form of reality checking we have; to see ourselves as others see us is the most illuminating form of self-knowledge we can gain, and also cheap at the price — such reflected truth can save us a lot of the pain we would endure if we had to discover truth at first hand.[18]

Our facade can be made smaller by self-disclosure, or giving feedback.[19] Why should you bother to do such a risky thing? For a start, self-disclosing may actually help you to clarify and formulate your own thoughts and feelings: 'How do I know what I think until I hear what I say?' Also, most people have a strong need to communicate with others, to 'get it off their chest' and not to 'bottle things up'. When this need cannot be met by actual interaction with others, people may self-disclose by keeping a diary, or talking to a pet, or talking to God. Self-disclosure can be used to project a favourable impression, as when we selectively self-disclose when out on a date with someone we are trying to impress, or when we are being interviewed for a job or promotion. Further, when we self-disclose, this acts as a model for others, and may lead to more open communication — 'I'll lower my Facade if you lower yours.' Finally, we should make a conscious effort to self-disclose because, as we have noted earlier, we may already be self-disclosing through slips of the tongue and body language.

Different windows: bulls, confessors, and others

The Johari Window can come in many different shapes. Different people have different windows, and indeed the one person might have different windows in different situations with different people.[20] Thus for example, Person A in figure 5.2 is a *mystery person*: these people don't give feedback about themselves, and they don't seek out feedback. Such people may have perfect self-knowledge and therefore don't need to interact with the world, but this seems unlikely, judging from the size of their Unknown area.

Person B is like a *bull in a china shop*: these people are very forward in giving feedback — opinions, feelings, thoughts — but don't appear to be too ready to accept feedback. They may not listen well, they may have behaved in such ways in the past — getting angry, bursting into tears, threatening to leave — that others have learned not to try very hard in giving feedback. Thus their Blind Spot is enormous.

Like Person B, Person C also indulges in one-way instead of two-way communication, but this time it is a different game: while these people ask for a lot of feedback ('What do you think?' 'How would you handle it if you were me?'), they give away very little about themselves. They want others to take risks, but do not wish to reciprocate. They play the role of *interviewer*, when in fact they should be playing the role of conversationalist, who gives as well as takes. The interviewer's Facade is thus very high.

Person D is very much into two-way communication, but at overkill levels. The *confessor* self-discloses just about everything about him/herself to others, and asks for continual feedback, but does not grasp that others are embarrassed or simply put off by such runaway feedback. The confessor's Blind Spot is large, and his/her Facade is — for other people's liking — too low.

Person E has an *ideal* window. These people have a low Facade (but not too low) and while they still have a Blind Spot, it is not large. As a consequence, their Arena is large, and their Unknown area is small. Such a person is easy to communicate with, and others rarely have to read their minds to find out what they really think and feel. Their self-knowledge is considerable.

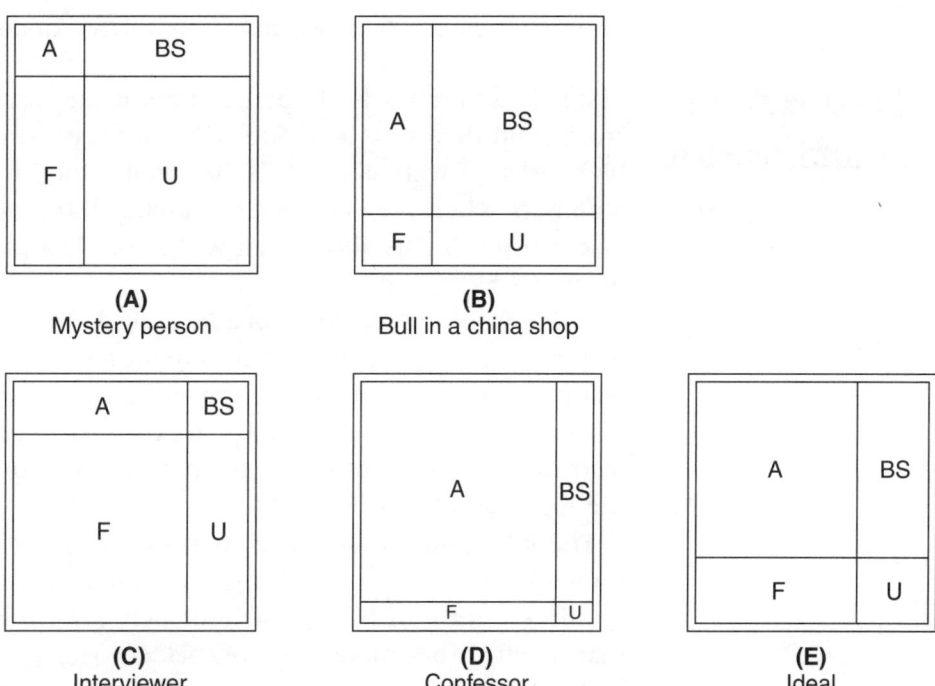

(A)
Mystery person

(B)
Bull in a china shop

(C)
Interviewer

(D)
Confessor

(E)
Ideal

Figure 5.2: Five different types of Johari Window

(Source: Reprinted and adapted from J. E. Jones and J. W. Pfeiffer (Eds.), *The 1973 Annual Handbook for Group Facilitators*, San Diego, CA: Pfeiffer & Company, 1973. Used with permission.)

Seeking and giving feedback: how to do it, when not to do it

Seeking feedback from others — so that we might see ourselves as others see us — is not easy, but it's not impossible. It's vital that you establish a norm in your own behaviour so that others know that they can tell you how they see you. Don't allow the situation to develop where the catchphrase of a breath freshener advertisement — even your best friends won't tell you — applies to you. Have yourself videotaped; you'll be surprised at what this can reveal about your verbal and non-verbal behaviour. Have friends or colleagues specifically observe you — for example, in meetings — and listen to their observations (you can do the same for them). Set up an anonymous suggestion system where you work. This can be risky but, after the silliness and abuse have been sifted away, some truths might emerge. Don't surround yourself with yes-people: be known as someone who is not afraid of the truth. Don't isolate yourself from others, particularly as you ascend the promotion ladder in work situations: nothing could be more cliched than the out-of-touch leader. Get into MBWA (Management by Walking Around).

Self-disclosure or giving feedback about yourself means expressing your opinions, feelings and thoughts in a manner appropriate to the situation. It is vital that group norms of conformity do not stifle such a free flow. In fact, it would be very useful to establish a norm of giving such frank feedback in a formal way — for example, a sound-off segment at the end of a team meeting when the formal business is concluded. Total truth in self-disclosure is, however, not necessary or even desirable. Sometimes even the frankest of communicators needs to tell white lies (to save face, to reduce tension or conflict) or to equivocate ('Well, this food certainly is — different!').[21] You need to make decisions about self-disclosure based upon your estimate of two inversely related quantities — risk and trust.

Feedback, risk and trust in teams

The risks and rewards of open communication are great in all human situations, and this is no less true when we are working in teams. There are high risks, as well as rewards, in placing total trust in your fellow team members when we consider the myths about and the politics of teams (see articles 'Myths about teamwork' (p. 47) and 'The internal politics of teams' (p. 59).

Going from the interpersonal level to the organisational level, there are major risk/trust problems: management has to trust that its investment in team training will not be compromised if workers leave abruptly to go elsewhere, while workers have to trust that their commitment to the restructuring inherent in the team model will not be repaid in layoffs at the first sign of problems.[22]

The Johari model shows us that rewards usually outweigh risks in substantially (but not totally) open communication. Such communication requires a norm of high trust, and such a norm is needed more in teams than in any other model of workplace organisation. Team members need to be able to identify and minimise those communication patterns or behaviours that inhibit the development of trust, while identifying and maximising those communication patterns or behaviours which facilitate the development of trust (see table 5.2).

Table 5.2: How to discourage and encourage trust in teams

BEHAVIOURS WHICH INHIBIT THE DEVELOPMENT OF TRUST	BEHAVIOURS WHICH FACILITATE THE DEVELOPMENT OF TRUST
When I see you doing these things, I tend to hide feelings, ideas and information from the team:	**If you want me to open up to you with my feelings, ideas and information, try any of these behaviours:**
Ridiculing	Smile at me
Lying	Spend some time small-talking with me about
Back stabbing	pleasant things
Using information against me	Look me in the eye
Acting in a two-faced manner	Have a good laugh with me
Ignoring	Listen to me
Pretending to be friendly	If you agree with me, say so
Neglecting tasks	Shake my hand
Gossiping	Welcome me
Withholding credit where credit is due	Confirm that you understand
Telling crude jokes	Include me in your activities
Embarrassing someone in front of the group	Clarify to make sure we understand each other
Interrupting	Encourage me by: patting me on the back; listening
Calling me or others names	to me; recognising me for something I've done
Constantly correcting or nit-picking	Find interests we have in common
Labelling people	Find experiences we have in common
Acting as if you know it all	Offer to help me
Trying too hard	Tell me about a similar situation you've been in
Making me feel dumb	Tell me another joke
Ordering people around all the time	Take a little risk
Expecting too much	Feel free to disagree with me, and give me the
Deserting me	same freedom
Controlling people excessively	Ask me for feedback
Acting inconsistently	Draw me a picture
Attacking	Cooperate with me
Avoiding eye-contact	Don't *always* disagree with me
Fidgeting	If you disagree, then criticise my ideas, not me
Dominating conversation	Tell me things that check out
Blaming	Go an extra mile
Saying 'yes, but ...' or 'no, but ...'	Share with me some more
Using obscene language	Reassure me when things aren't going well
Not listening	Sympathise with me
Using a tone of voice that's sarcastic, angry, loud,	Offer me constructive criticism
superior, harsh	Empathise; take the time to feel how I feel
Breaking promises	Get to know me
Playing one-upmanship	Tell me things about my *behaviour* that you don't
Pushing people around	like
Passing judgement	Accept me for who I am
Failing to keep something confidential	Help me settle our conflicts
Giving up	Tell me I'm valuable to the team
Over-reacting when proved wrong	
Setting up someone for failure	
Not opening up to me	
Shooting down ideas	
Talking down to me	
Always having the last say	

(continued)

Table 5.2: How to discourage and encourage trust in teams (*continued*)

BEHAVIOURS WHICH INHIBIT THE DEVELOPMENT OF TRUST	BEHAVIOURS WHICH FACILITATE THE DEVELOPMENT OF TRUST
In general, I do not trust those people who show:	**In general, I will open up and trust those people who:**
An unwillingness to listen, an unwillingness to change, an unwillingness to compromise A lack of real interest or concern That they have little time for me A lack of real caring Open and prolonged hostility (or who permit this to go on in the team) Arrogance Little respect by keeping me in the dark about important changes or other events which affect me directly A closed mind, disrespect, mistrust, hostility, prejudice, inflexibility A tendency to criticise me or punish me excessively	Are honest with me Share with me Are sincere Explain it to me Keep their word Spend time with me Are genuine Identify with me Ask me a question Work with me on something Tell me a good joke Play with me (ping pong, darts, etc.) Talk to me Say hello Open up to me Ask me how it's going Offer me some more help Ask me another question Forgive my mistakes Say: 'I like you.'

(Source: Mink, Mink and Owen (1987: 74, 76). Reproduced with permission.)

The Johari Window is extremely useful for analysing the manner in which individuals seek feedback about themselves and give out feedback about themselves. Let's expand the model to include seeking feedback from others and giving feedback to others (figure 5.3). Such a model gives us a visual introduction to two skills: the skill of giving feedback, and the skill of listening.

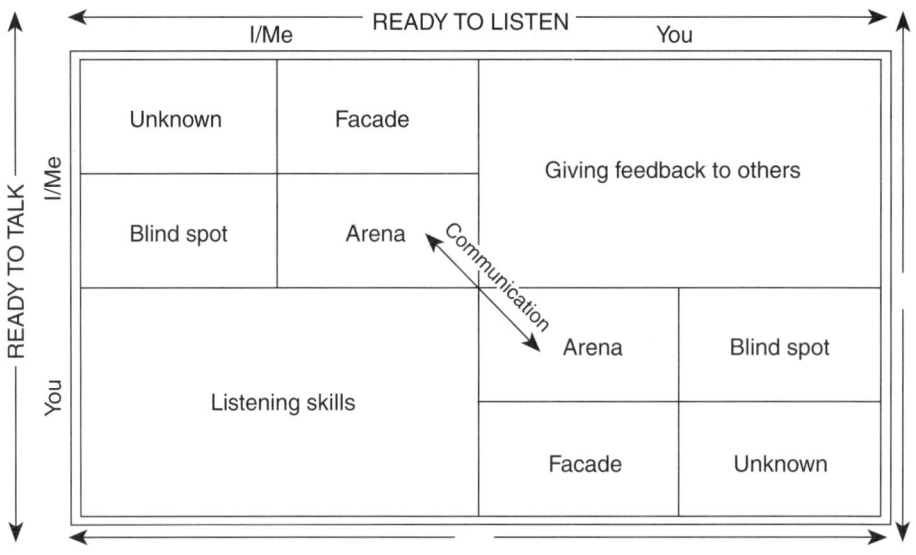

Figure 5.3: An expanded model of feedback in communication

T A L K I N G
P O I N T S

GUIDELINES TO STIFLING COMMUNICATION

The following points are guaranteed to *discourage* communication. Can you think of any others?

1. Do not adhere to the KISS principle (Keep it simple, stupid).
2. Use only the language of lawyers and bureaucrats.
3. Only communicate vertically, up the line.
4. Only communicate facts, never opinions.
5. Only communicate good news and remember to grab all the credit that's going.
6. Delegate the communication of bad news.
7. Where possible communicate by letter, memos and so on; never verbally unless you really have to.
8. Do not allocate a specific time for team briefings.
9. Discourage verbal comprehension by belittling the questioner.
10. Treat team members as immature in any communications with them (make some time to practise talking down to people).
11. Always use politics as an excuse for not being open and honest with your team.
12. Ridicule new ideas from below and treat them with suspicion.
13. Criticise freely and withhold recognition and praise.
14. Regard all problems as failures, and discourage people drawing problems to your attention.
15. Using I.T. (Information Technology) systems, restrict information flows with hierarchical passwords.
16. Regard open communications by management down the line as a dismissable offence.
17. Take every opportunity you can to distance yourself from company initiatives, especially those to do with communications.
18. Re-state the company rules as often as possible, using the company noticeboards.
19. Ask departments and teams to challenge and criticise each other's proposals.
20. In meetings, always encourage in-fighting and praise the winner.

(Source: John Spencer and Adrian Pruss, *Managing Your Team: How to Organise People for Maximum Results* (London, Piatkus, 1992), pp. 131–32. Reproduced with permission.)

GIVING FEEDBACK: A SEQUENCE MODEL

Making sure we express our feelings to other team members sounds like a good idea, but many of us would be uncomfortable doing it. Let's look at a simple sequence model for giving feedback that can help to remove a lot of the stress and initial awkwardness involved.[23] An overview of the model is shown in table 5.3 overleaf.

Table 5.3: A feedback model

1.	When you ... (do something)
2.	This happens ...
3.	And I feel ...
4.	Would you ... (do something else)
5.	Because/that way/this would mean ...
6.	I/you/they would feel ...
7.	So what do you think?

Initially, there are four styles of interpersonal communication that should be distinguished:

1. Aggression
2. Passivity
3. Manipulativeness
4. Assertiveness.

The first three styles are flawed — they are ineffective, stressful and counterproductive. You should strive to develop an assertive style when interacting with others.[24] Let's look at examples of all four styles in operation within the sequence model of giving feedback.

Table 5.4: Giving feedback: a sequence model

Feedback phase	Feedback: words to use	Example	Behavioural style	Analysis
1	When you ...	When you arrive late for meetings, like today ...	Assertive	Specific and descriptive — an impartial observer would be able to confirm that this behaviour occurred.
		When you were arriving late for meetings last month ...	Passive	Why procrastinate so long in complaining? Delaying means that you have been stewing on the problem, and the other person has presumed that lateness is okay with you.
		When you eventually do get around to putting in an appearance at meetings ...	Aggressive	Sarcasm puts the other person on the defensive, and you send the message that you don't really want to solve the problem, merely deliver abuse.

Feedback phase	Feedback: words to use	Example	Behavioural style	Analysis
1 (cont.)		You're always late for meetings . . .	Aggressive	Absolutes like 'always' and 'never' polarise the situation: the other person either has nowhere to hide, and no way to save face, negotiate or solve the problem, or else they will retaliate with nit-picking — 'I was early on the 14th . . .' which again leads away from problem-solving.
		People around here are getting pretty fed up with the situation . . .	Passive/ manipulative	Are they? Have they been struck dumb? Let them speak for themselves, and you speak for yourself. These words are so abstract — how about some people-names in there, like 'I' and 'you'?
		You're totally useless . . .	Aggressive	Possible, but unlikely. Condemning people for their personality is like telling them that you don't like them because they're too short or too tall: there's nothing they can do to please you. If you refer to specific behaviour only, you give them freedom to move and the chance to change that behaviour.
2	This happens . . .	We can't get the total team's input . . .	Assertive	Specific and descriptive — shows impact or consequences of behaviour upon you and the team.
		You must show up to meetings or you will be punished . . .	Aggressive	Inflicting punishment, like taking revenge, is a cheap thrill that often proves to be very expensive. Why? Because punishment doesn't work all that well as a strategy to change people's behaviour, and should only be used in extreme circumstances. Punishing an individual may call forth resentment and retaliation from the individual, and may damage the non-authoritarian, we're-all-equals culture that effective teams usually have.

(continued)

Table 5.4: Giving feedback: a sequence model (*continued*)

Feedback phase	Feedback: words to use	Example	Behavioural style	Analysis
2 (cont.)		Things don't go as well as they should	Passive	Evasive, pussy-footing and hopelessly vague. Again, the Passive's flight into the abstract and depersonalised.
		You ought to be more reliable . . .	Aggressive	Yes, and we should all be perfect — but we're not. Moralising like this implies that your morals are superior, and will block communication and lessen your influence. Aggressives really should stop using 'should', 'ought', and 'must' so often — and they should stop wagging and pointing their index fingers.
3	And I feel . . .	. . . and I feel really frustrated	Assertive	Clear statement of your feelings.
		Silence	Passive	Passives will go silent here, because of their avoidance of 'I' statements. The stress they might feel at letting people know they have feelings is nothing compared to the stress they put themselves through in bottling up such feelings.
		You make me get stressed.	Passive	Other people do not control us so much: they influence, but are not responsible for, our feelings. This is victim-talk. Use the 'I' word.
		More 'you have sinned' messages; no 'I' messages	Aggressive	'I' messages create an adult/peer relationship, and the other person is more likely to listen. Nothing but 'you' messages calls forth defensiveness, and the other person is less likely to hear what you are saying.
		I'm a bit annoyed . . . I'm just a little irritated by this . . .	Passive	Don't be surprised then if the other person only changes 'a little' or 'a bit'. Modifiers are used here out of fear — used presumably to appease the other person, and prevent them from losing their temper. However, modifiers weaken your message, trivialise the issue (So what's the problem?) and are an exercise in self-humiliation.

Feedback phase	Feedback: words to use	Example	Behavioural style	Analysis
4	Would you …	Would you be able to re-schedule your commitments elsewhere so that you can get here on time?	Assertive	Positive solution suggested. No loaded language. Dignity of other person not compromised, so there's no need for them to get defensive.
		Would you be able to get your act into gear and get here on time for a change?	Aggressive	Have you stopped beating your wife? There are real questions, to which multiple responses are possible, and rhetorical or trick questions, to which there is no dignified response. This is not a real question, and sarcasm is the cheapest of thrills.
5	Because/ That way/ This would mean …	This would mean that the team meeting could achieve more, and then we could all get back to our individual work that much quicker.	Assertive	Solution-oriented, and answers questions everyone asks, or thinks: 'What's in it for me?' 'What's the payoff for changing my behaviour?' This is the task-oriented incentive.
		That way we could at least shut the chairman up and keep the others happy. It's no skin off my nose, but let's not make waves.	Manipulative	Compromise and politics have their place, but not here. Honesty and directness, not deviousness, is needed here. With Manipulatives, it's wise to remember that if they conspire with, they will conspire against, you; if they gossip to you, they will gossip about you.
6	I/You/They would feel …	I would feel a lot better about the situation. So would the team. So would you, I'm sure.	Assertive	This is the socio-emotional incentive. It's important to switch back from the logical, problem-solving dimension to the feelings dimension, to show that the drama and conflict being experienced can be resolved.
7	So what do you think?	So what do you think?	Assertive	Neutral, non-confrontational — an equal-to-equal expression. Shows you are willing to listen.

(Source: Feedback Model adapted from *The Team Handbook* © 1988 Joiner Associates Inc. all rights reserved, and from *Working Together*, Bob Montgomery (1986, Thomas Nelson). Adapted by the author with permission.)

The feedback model gives us a structure for expressing feelings and resolving conflict within the team. Remember, when you first start to use it, it may feel artificial and silly, but persevere, and you will find it a very useful tool of assertive communication. Rehearsal in front of a mirror, video camera and/or friends can improve your technique and also make you feel a good deal more comfortable with it. Rehearsal also means that in the real or perceived stress of a confrontation with the target of your feedback, you can put some of your thinking brain on automatic pilot while your new memories of the sequence play back through you.

When you go through the sequence, look directly at the person who is the target of the feedback — if you avert your gaze, you are sending out multiple and contradictory messages. Remember, you are expressing the way you feel — not the way you think, or the ways in which others might feel or think. This is your perfect right to express this, just as it is the perfect right of others to use the sequence when talking to you.

So much for giving feedback to others. But what happens when others are talking, and we are listening? The next section looks at the skills of listening, which are not quite as obvious as you might think.

QUESTIONS, QUESTIONS ...

1. If you were to detect some incongruence between a person's words and their non-verbal behaviour (e.g., behaviour suggesting rage, frustration, disapproval), how would you broach this with the person?
2. What non-verbal behaviour would you expect to see in (a) an effective team (b) an ineffective team?
3. How might standards of self-disclosure vary:
   • between different individuals?
   • between different groups?
   • between different cultures?
4. How would you best handle people who gave you passive, aggressive or manipulative feedback?
5. Use the feedback sequence model to devise some positive feedback — for example, complimenting someone on their outstanding performance.

BARRIERS TO EFFECTIVE LISTENING: GAMES LISTENERS PLAY

There are a number of specific behaviour patterns which present barriers to effective listening. These are, in effect, mind games played by people who do not listen well. They are Games Listeners Play.[25]

Some of these barriers are expressed in the words used by bad listeners. Some of the barriers are not visible to us because they are comprised of thoughts or 'self-talk'.[26] Some of the barriers are simply non-verbal — the 'go away' or 'I'm just not tuned in' signals of the glassy stare, the sphinx-like immobile face, the drumming fingers, the glance at a watch or clock on the wall, the pen held suspended over documents deemed to be more interesting than your conversation, the body oriented away, the barriers of a large desk, a hostile secretary, and an over-full appointments book — truly, the silent language of non-verbal communication can sometimes be deafening.

Most people are guilty of erecting such barriers every now and then, but there is no malign intent involved, and no great harm done. The real damage is done by bad listeners who erect one, several or all of these barriers all the time. Let's stroll through the behavioural zoo and examine such barriers.

1. Subject changing

Occurs when a listener feels bored, embarrassed or threatened by what the speaker is saying.

2. Identifying

Similar to subject changing: the listener throws the speaker off by relating everything back to the listener's own experiences, which they insist on recounting in detail.

3. Daydreaming

Occurs when the listener does not creatively exploit the gap between speaking rate and listening rate by analysing the speaker's words, but instead allows the speaker's words to trigger off an associated thought, and then drifts off to a progressively more remote series of associations — until they have lost track entirely of what the speaker is saying. The daydreamer's train of thought is a runaway train.

4. Just gimme the facts

Facts are vital to understanding, but listeners also need to detect feelings, values, implicit meanings (read or heard 'between the lines'), and non-verbal behaviour, which may confirm or contradict facts expressed in words. The JGTF listener, feeling that anything non-factual is thus fictitious, thereby misses entire dimensions of meaning.

5. Mind-reading

The direct opposite of JGTF. Occurs when a listener attempts to read too much meaning into feelings, values, implicit meanings and non-verbal behaviour in a misguided attempt to detect what the speaker is 'really saying', ignoring plain facts and clear words.

6. Rehearsing

Occurs when a person is angered by what she/he is hearing, and concentrates so hard on a detailed rebuttal that they lose track of what is currently being said. Also occurs when a listener is planning witty or profound responses. The listener might rehearse entire chains of responses: 'I'll say . . . then she'll say . . . then I'll say . . .'.

7. Comparing

Occurs where the listener is insecure, competitive, envious or jealous, or all of these. Loses track of, or misinterprets, what the speaker is saying because listener continually compares his/her situation with theirs: 'I make more than that ... what would I need to do to speak like that? ... my daughter gets better marks than that ... How can he afford those clothes?'

8. Hit my buttons

Many people lose their cool and objectivity and become extremely sensitive when certain topics are broached by speakers ('crime, abortion, capital punishment, Islam, taxation, politics'). In fact, their reaction is so automatic, unthinking and predictable, that it is almost as if someone had just pushed a button in their brain. Fine for robots, but bad for effective listeners, conversationalists and problem-solvers.

9. Stereotyping

Similar to HMB, except that here the listener ignores the words being said because she/he takes exception to the speaker's hairstyle, clothing, sex, socio-economic class, mannerisms, race, religion, sexual preference, approach to the topic, use of audio-visual aids or any one of a number of factors that do not have much to do with the ideas being expressed.

10. Quick fix

Some people are fortunate enough to have the solutions to everyone's problems, and they can detect a speaker's problem after only a few words or sentences have been uttered — at which point they cut the speaker off and give them a detailed program of what to do now. Such listeners ignore the feelings of speakers, and can't grasp the notion that sometimes people don't want quick fixes — they just want people to listen and just *be* there.

To check your understanding of these barriers, complete Exercise E.

EXERCISE

**E:
BARRIERS TO
COMMUNICATION**

Match up the barriers to effective listening in the left-hand column with the examples in the right-hand column. Note that S = spoken words, and T = thoughts.

1. Subject changing

A (T) He thinks he's got problems — I've handled worse than that.

2. Identifying

B (T) I really couldn't care less about this computer stuff ... wish they were as simple as my home computer ... the games are such fun ... Gee, that was fun when we played those games at the arcade last night ... I wonder if she likes me? ...

3. Daydreaming

C (S) Yeah, sure, I'll do it later — oh, by the way, can I talk to you while you're here about the Brazilian contract ...

4. Just gimme the facts

D (S) Sorry to jump in, but I think I've got the picture already. I think you should just leave him — he's obviously no good for you.

5. Mindreading

E (S) You know, that reminds me of something very similar that happened to me. Let me fill you in on the background. Many years ago ...

6. Rehearsing

F (T) What a moron. How could you believe someone who can't even dry-clean her outfit. And if she doesn't stop playing with those pearls, I'll scream.

7. Comparing

G (T) Hmm ... he paused before he said '... and the Sales Department.' What does that mean? And he folded his arms when he mentioned budget cuts. Is he really saying that my area's in trouble?

8. Hit my buttons

H (T) Well now ... 53 per cent down, eh? Surely seasonal adjustments wouldn't account for all of that ... damn, she's pushed that overhead askew. We'll have to renegotiate that before penalties cut in ... What? She's crying? Now what brought *that* on?

9. Stereotyping

I (T) Hah, well I've got him there. I've got the figures here that will destroy that argument. I'll start off with the 1990 figures; I'll get in a dig there about his division's performance, and then I'll ...

10. Quick fix

J (T) Capital punishment? You stand there and casually say that capital punishment might be justified in *some* circumstances? I've got to shut you up *now*. (S) ...

• •

ACTIVE LISTENING

When people erect barriers to effective listening, then they sometimes move beyond the passivity of simply receiving a spoken message (and various non-verbal messages) and into the active role of speaker themselves — a sure sign of ineffectiveness.

Yet it is possible to be an effective listener and not be merely a passive receiver — in fact, it is not only possible, but desirable and necessary. Communication simply cannot be a one-way process, wherein someone sends a message and we absorb it like a sponge. Many messages can be distorted in the sending and in the receiving, and unless we check back with the sender of the message, communication may have broken down without one or both parties being aware of it.

We may need to move from passive listening to *active listening*, which is a communication skill pioneered by psychologist Carl Rogers.[27] The concept of active listening may initially seem to be a contradiction in terms, but listening is not simply hearing — it involves concentration, attention and comprehension.

Perhaps truly effective listening involves responding as well: not in the full-blown sense within a conversation, where the listener switches roles to that of speaker, and sends a new message back to the former speaker/current listener, but more in the partial sense, where the listener can help the speaker clarify the message being sent, and help explore the emotional dimensions of that message. As Mortimer Adler puts it:

> *The most prevalent mistake that people make about listening is to regard it as passively receiving rather than as actively participating ... Catching is as much an activity as throwing and requires as much skill, though it is a skill of a different kind. Without the complementary efforts of both players ... the play cannot be completed.*[28]

Clarifying

To avoid this distortion in the communication process, it is often useful to simply check with the speaker as to what they really meant by using certain clarifying phrases, such as:

- What I think you said was . . .
- What I hear you saying is . . .
- What specifically do you mean by . . .?
- Let me just check this with you. You think that . . . (restatement/summary). Is that right?

If the listener clarifies with the original speaker, and the speaker agrees that that is what she or he actually meant, then both have confirmation that good and clear communication has taken place. If the listener clarifies with the original speaker, and the speaker disagrees that that is what she or he actually meant, then both speaker and listener now have the chance to confirm what the undistorted original message was, to the satisfaction of both parties — and again, good and clear communication has taken place.

Closed and open questions

As you move on from simply checking out the realities of a situation, you may find it useful to draw out the speaker more. To interrogate someone is offensive, not to mention counter-productive (because it evokes defensive and hostile responses). Yet many people inadvertently interrogate people because they ask closed rather than open questions (table 5.5).

Closed questions are those that require a simple yes/no response, whereas open questions are those that can evoke a wide range of responses. Although closed questions often have a place in particular areas of communication, such as in items on a questionnaire (so that simple responses from many people can be collated to detect an overall trend), they are often a cause of frustrating dead-ends in normal conversation, because once the person asked the questions has answered either 'yes' or 'no', nothing more is required of them. The questioner has — rather arrogantly — limited the alternatives for the person being questioned, whereas, in fact, there may not be two but 392 alternatives — as the questioned person sees things. The conversation also ends up sounding like an interrogation, or a series of ultimatums, which gives both parties feelings of futility and tension.

In getting deeper and more meaningful responses from people, and in order to make the two-way communication process really work, you should strive to ask open questions more often.

Table 5.5: Samples of open and closed questions

Closed question	Open question
• Did you like your last job?	• What did you like or dislike about your last job?
• Do you love her?	• How do you feel about her?
• Are you unhappy?	• What's on your mind?
• Do you want to go there?	• Where would you like to go?

Reflecting and paraphrasing

Sometimes, simple clarifying and open questions are not enough, particularly when the speaker is expressing strong negative emotions. To simply check the facts of the case may be as insensitive as erecting a *just gimme the facts* listening barrier.

An effective response in circumstances like these is to simply reflect back the feelings or perceptions to the person who is angry, depressed or anxious, sometimes by paraphrasing what the person has just said, or putting what they have just said into your own words. This takes a bit of practice, and you may feel awkward doing it at first, because if it is not done with real empathy and sensitivity towards the other person, it sounds like mere parroting or mimicking, which the other person will find offensive, and communication will break down totally. The advantages of this reflective listening are:

1. The other person feels that you have understood the facts, but you are also aware of his/her emotions.

2. You haven't begun a new train or thought or message of your own, but are encouraging the other person to pursue his/her original train of thought: you haven't cramped their personal style.

3. You are not sitting in judgement on them: you grant them the compliment of understanding.

This does not necessarily mean that you agree with what you are hearing — you may, in fact, express disagreement later. Keep in mind the following: 'Ironically, the less we judge speakers, the more apt they are to become self-critical, expressing their thoughts and feelings even more honestly than if they felt under scrutiny.'[29]

Styles of response

Reflective listening is one of five styles of response that people commonly adopt when they are in the role of listening to other people talking.[30] These styles are:

1. Judgemental/evaluative/moralistic
The receiver of the message has made a judgement of the merit or otherwise of the message sender's words, and has a clear idea of what the sender should now do.

2. Interpretive/explanatory/analysing
The receiver wishes to teach or show the sender the 'real purpose' or 'hidden meaning' of the message, and what the sender should now do.

3. Supportive/soothing/sympathetic/reassuring
The receiver wishes to soothe the sender's feelings and reduce the intensity of those feelings.

4. Probing/questioning/information gathering
The receiver wishes to obtain further information from the sender, with a view to solving the factual problem of the sender.

5. Empathic/understanding/reflecting/paraphrasing
The receiver only wishes to clarify and show understanding of the factual and emotional dimensions of the sender's message.

Carl Rogers argues that these five responses comprise 80 per cent of all messages sent between individuals (the other 20 per cent being incidental and of no great importance). He found that the different responses were used in the following order (most frequently to least frequently):

1. Evaluative
2. Interpretive
3. Supportive
4. Probing
5. Understanding.

Rogers also suggested that if a person uses one type of response as much as 40 per cent of the time, then other people see him/her as *always* responding in that way.

All of these styles have their value, and can be used in different listening situations. The understanding style, however, is the only style that does not shift the focus away from the speaker to the listener, and may thus inhibit the speaker in the current conversation and also inhibit communication between speaker and listener in the long run. Which is your dominant style? Find out now by looking at Exercise F. Further insights into the five styles are given in table 5.6.

EXERCISE

**F:
LISTENING AND
RESPONDING**

Read the statements of the following four different people. Imagine you are having a conversation with each of them. Of the five responses, choose the one that is closest to the way you would respond. (See table 5.6 for an analysis of your choice.)

Statement 1

Barry: I'm really freaking out about this exam. I just know I'm going to fail it.

- A. Snap out of it — you've always got through before.
- B. You're feeling pretty stressed about this, then.
- C. I feel for you — but it'll soon be over.
- D. Don't you think that if you studied a bit more this wouldn't happen?
- E. What parts of the paper do you think you'll fail on?

Statement 2

Celia: I shouldn't have bought this dress on credit. My husband will kill me.

- A. Why do you think you used your credit card again?
- B. I wouldn't be surprised if he does kill you — you know you can't afford it.
- C. I know how you feel. I've done that kind of thing myself and instantly regretted it.
- D. You're really worried your husband won't understand?
- E. You probably did it because you were depressed and wanted something to brighten you up.

Statement 3

Jane: I just don't know what to do with Brian. He's so incompetent. I think I've got no alternative but to sack him, but I hate doing that kind of thing.

- A. You're so right. He's nothing but a loser.
- B. You're annoyed because he makes your department look bad; is that it?
- C. You sound quite frustrated. Some of your staff are letting you down, and forcing you to consider options that aren't your style.
- D. Just ignore him — it's not worth getting upset over. It'll work out, you'll see.
- E. What specifically has he been doing wrong?

Statement 4

Peter: The relationship just can't go on. I think I'm going to have to leave her. What should I do?

- A. Don't worry. I'm sure things will work out if you just give her some more time.
- B. Is there anyone else you could start a relationship with if you drop her?
- C. Get rid of her. Don't give it a second thought.
- D. You wouldn't have to go through this drama if you'd only think more before getting involved.
- E. Mary and you have got problems and it might be the end, eh?

Key to Exercise F

Style	1. Judgemental	2. Interpretive	3. Supportive	4. Probing	5. Understanding
Statement 1	A	D	C	E	B
Statement 2	B	E	C	A	D
Statement 3	A	B	D	E	C
Statement 4	C	D	A	B	E

Table 5.6: Summary of response styles

Response	1. Judgemental	2. Interpretive	3. Supportive	4. Probing	5. Understanding
Description	• Judgemental • Evaluative • Advice-giving	• Interpretive • Explanatory	• Supporting • Reassuring	• Probing • Exploratory • Questioning • Information-seeking	• Understanding • Empathising • Reflecting • Paraphrasing
Response	'I think you should . . .'	'You do that because . . .'	'Never mind, it's bound to get better.'	'When did you first feel that way?'	'You sound really happy.'
Intentions	• To make a judgement on the goodness/ badness, rightness/ wrongness • To tell the other person what he or she should/should not do • To put things right	• To explain the cause • To tell the meaning • To teach the other person	• To reassure • To minimise feeling • To soften the blow • To avoid intense feeling	• To seek more information • To tell the speaker what is okay or important to talk about	• To check whether responder understands accurately • To clarify what has been said • To stay close to the here and now experience of the speaker • To understand and share

Response	1. Judgemental	2. Interpretive	3. Supportive	4. Probing	5. Understanding
Possible effects	• May create distrust • May be helpful when judgement is asked for • Sets the responder above the speaker as more authoritative • Says to speaker: 'I know more about your situation than you do and this is how you should act' • May put the speaker on the defensive leading to resentment, closing up, resistance, argument • Moves the focus from the speaker to the responder • Says some feelings are not okay • Leads to censoring • Limits communication	• Sets the responder above the speaker as wiser, more clever and better informed • Gives information/ insight — seldom leads to change • Intellectualises the conversation, moving it away from feelings • Moves focus from speaker to responder. Can help. Usually doesn't	• Makes speaker feel more secure, less alone • May leave speaker feeling not understood • Minimises feelings • May indicate that feelings are temporary • May encourage avoidance of feelings • May give speaker false sense of security and reduce efforts for change • Shifts focus from speaker to responder	• Gives more information to responder • May open up new aspects for speaker and lead to clarification • Moves topic away from here-and-now experience • May make both people feel safer • Intellectualises conversation from feelings to facts • Moves focus from what speaker wants to say to what listener wants to know • May block the conversation and shut the speaker up	• Encourages speaker to continue the exploration of feelings and ideas further • Communicates acceptance and concern to the speaker • Communicates respect • Speaker feels understood, less lonely, more self-accepting, less self-deprecating, more aware of own value, more free to act appropriately when ready

Note: Often one response mixes a number of intentions and may fit more than one category.

(Source: Anne Kotzman, *Listen to Me, Listen to You: A Practical Guide to Improving Self-Esteem, Listening Skills and Assertiveness* (Penguin, Ringwood, Victoria, 1989), pp. 50–51. Reproduced with permission.)

JARGON

We have covered a lot of ground in considering the more subtle dimensions of communication, such as non-verbal communication, feedback of various kinds, and listening. Now let's return to what should be the more predictable world of words, used in normal everyday transactions between team members. — 'should be', but not necessarily 'is'.

Communication can obviously only take place if people share meanings. Yet even when people are speaking the same language, communication can break down when they are speaking different sub-languages, such as slang or jargon. Jargon is a particular problem for teams, both for communication within the team and communication from the team to the outside world.

Jargon is specialised technical language, and there are as many different jargons as there are professions and specialisations within those professions. Jargon usually starts out innocently enough as abbreviations, shorthand descriptions of things — 'We'll need to TOK that leftie unit before the tenth floor starts snooping around at the end of the month.' Like all secret languages, however, jargon takes on a behavioural, as well as a technical or convenience, function — it shows who is in the in-group, and it acts as a device to exclude all those in the out-group.

Team members need to be aware that 'outsiders' do not share some meanings of words, phrases, abbreviations and acronyms with them, and that, therefore, when communicating with the outside world, care should be taken to 'translate' (without patronising or talking down to people).

Similarly, within groups there may be a jargon problem: increasingly, teams are composed of specialists from different areas, and all are dependent upon others to speak in a neutral, common language if understanding and effectiveness are to prevail.

If such neutral common language does not prevail within groups and in the group's communications to the outside world, then dangerous language games may be being played: the offending individual or in-group values the satisfactions of exclusivity above the satisfactions of effectiveness — clearly a selfish, and self-defeating, strategy.

Individuals and groups sometimes say that it is impossible to communicate 'down' to the level of 'outsiders' because of the sheer marvellous complexity and inner logic of their secret domain — but if money and resources appear to be drying up because of this inability to communicate, it's remarkable how quickly 'translations' can be forthcoming.

Also, as we have seen in chapter 2, there is a phenomenon in groups known as 'Groupthink', whereby groups find the internal dynamics of groups so satisfying that they begin to seriously misperceive what is happening in the outside world. The over-use of jargon is often seen in groups suffering from Groupthink.

How difficult is it for newcomers to a group to understand its jargon? Try Exercise G, which follows.

EXERCISE

G: TRANSLATING JARGON

1. Gather together some friends, colleagues or team members.
2. Each person should get up and address the group, talking about an area they have some skill or expertise in. This might be work-related, or it might be a hobby or interest. Each person should give a 1–2 minute talk *twice* — once with all the obscure jargon they can think of, and once without.
3. All group members, including the speaker, should share their perceptions of the two versions of each talk. How much difference was there? Did the jargon-free version take longer? Were there certain words or concepts that were 'untranslatable'?
4. All group members should now share an experience they have had of jargon in other situations, either as perpetrator or victim. Have there ever been any communication breakdowns, even among fellow jargon users?
5. How might groups develop norms or procedures to help manage specialised language?

TALKING POINTS **YOU DON'T SAY?** Still more of what people say about groups and teams

It's a very difficult job, so the only way to succeed is to work together as a team. And that means that you do exactly as I say.

Charlie Croker (Michael Caine),
***The Italian Job**, by Troy Kennedy Martin*

Teams alone can't effect change. You must have a change in corporate culture. You don't get involvement and commitment with perks. The sacred cows (of motivation) have no place in work teams.

Rob Burch,
Steelcase Canada Ltd

Communicate. When he was still part of the Carter administration, Alfred Kahn addressed a conference on communication with this classic opening line: 'I will not communicate with you. I will talk to you.'

Feedback. This word, along with input, has become so overworked that Provost John McCall of the University of Cincinnati received national attention when he ruled that any administrator who used either of these words in university communications would be fined two bits.

Junk Words (Contemporary Clichés') Paul Dickson,
Dickson's Word Treasury

The modern working man feels the need of belonging to a team.

Pehr G. Gyllenhammar,
Managing Director, Volvo

Organising for innovation means flattening the hierarchy, giving responsibility to the lower levels, scuttling discipline-oriented departments in favour of ad hoc mission team groups.

Michael Dertouzos,
Chairman,
Massachusetts Institute of Technology
Productivity Commission

The popular wisdom of mangement theory is that every individual can find or be helped to find a 'role' in groups. I suggest the opposite, that all individuals experience substantial and continuing internal tensions as group members, that participation in groups is usually stressful and only occasionally, for some, satisfying. This tension derives from individual needs to establish special relationships with the leader, a need which groups inevitably frustrate. Recent research on industrial democracy programs supports the argument that participation in work groups can often be a source of stress rather than satisfaction. Certain types of workers and certain types of work seem better suited to solitary work environments. Research reveals that individuals with particular work styles will perform poorly in the team.

Amanda Sinclair,
Melbourne University Graduate School
of Management

I see us moving towards a team-oriented, multi-skilled environment in which the team takes on many of the supervisor's and trainer's tasks. If you combine that with some sort of gain sharing, you probably will have a much more productive plant with higher employee satisfaction and commitment.

Robert Haas,
CEO, Levi-Strauss

The team concept is more than a mere gimmick; it is an attempt by management to control not only the worker's behaviour on the job, but also the worker's feelings and thoughts. The employer plays upon the worker's desire to use his or her creativity or intellect. The team concept promises that he or she will be something more than a mere factory hand, calls upon him to think, and asks him to cooperate with management.

But cooperation with management ever so subtly turns into competition with one's fellow workers. In the struggle for productivity and even quality, department is pitted against department, and worker is pitted against worker. What began by appealing to the worker's idealism turns some workers into informers and weakens union solidarity. Often when workers are reluctant to approve the team approach, they are threatened by management with plant closings.

Victor Reuther,
one of the founders of the (US) United Auto Workers

Advances in service quality today rely heavily on an organisation's ability to discover ways of increasing the responsiveness to customers and the marketplace — the days of the 'standard model' are long over. In searching for ways to adapt more quickly, many companies are realising the inherent advantages of work teams. Teams can communicate better, tackle more opportunities, find better solutions, and implement actions more quickly. Many teams in manufacturing environments are organised into work 'cells', which reorganise in a fluid way to accommodate shifting demands in production. Because of the nature of teams, their members are often more engaged, alert, proactive, knowledgeable and generally better able to respond to varying conditions than traditionally organised workforces.

Richard S. Wellins, William C. Byham and Jean M. Wilson,
Empowered Teams

In management and union circles, as well as the popular press, the system we have described as management-by-stress is referred to as the 'team concept' . . . In the actual operation of the plant — as opposed to the ideological hype — 'teams' is simply the name management gives to its administrative units. For the most part, if we substituted 'supervisor's sub-group' for team and 'sub-group leader' for team-leader, understanding of management-by-stress would not suffer at all.

There is, however, some reality to the popular notions about teams. Some teams meet and discuss real problems. When the line moves slowly enough workers can and do help each other out. But this is most likely during initial start-up when the 'teams' often consist mainly of supervisors, engineers and team leaders. Once the line is up to speed, jobs are specified in detail and each worker can barely keep up with his or her own job, let alone help someone else out. Besides, the system does not like regular initiative or uncharted actions on the line. When the system is running at regular production speed, team meetings tend to drop in frequency.

Mike Parker and Jane Slaughter,
Choosing Sides

For all individuals, group life creates conflict between seeking the satisfaction of belonging and a sense of frustration at having to conform.

W. R. Bion

The abilities of teams to solve problems are often . . . in inverse proportion to the amount of information needed to do so.

John Spencer and Adrian Pruss

A 'team' may be defined as a group of persons connected by agreed-upon objectives and tasks. The team's functions may be carried out by the total group, by a sub-group, or by individuals having the support and resources of groups available to them.

Eva Schindler-Rainman

MYTH NO. 8: TEAM CONCEPT BRINGS THE FEELING OF TEAMWORK ON THE SHOP FLOOR.

In fact the overloaded jobs under team concept serve to prevent workers from helping each other. Team concept tries to break down the solidarity and teamwork of natural work groups that develop on the shop floor, by trying — usually unsuccessfully — to channel that sentiment into formal, highly controlled, company-designed team structures.

Management says it wants to build 'worker loyalty', but top managers themselves are loyal only to their careers, not their companies. When workers join management's 'team' to beat the competition, they too often find that management has become a free agent and sold itself to a higher bidder. Dennis Pawley left one of GM's early team concept plants, to become plant manager at Mazda and then left Mazda for Otis Elevator

Mike Parker and Jane Slaughter,
Choosing Sides

Trust means: 'I know that you will not — deliberately or accidentally, consciously or unconsciously — take unfair advantage of me. I can put my situation at the moment, my status and self-esteem in this group, our relationship, my job, my career, even my life, in your hands with complete confidence'.

Douglas McGregor

Teams are here to stay. We cannot avoid them. Most of life is now too complicated to be dealt with by one woman or one man on their own. A good team is a great place to be — exciting, stimulating, supportive, successful. A bad team is horrible, a sort of human prison. We can make teams good if we understand them — they seldom happen that way by chance.

Charles Handy

... even for those who thrive on the group experience and perhaps enjoy their job more, does this necessarily lead to improved, in task terms, performance? A strong link between satisfaction and performance in the workplace has by no means been finally established. Observing work groups there is a good deal, sometimes a preponderance, of behaviour transacted which is clearly anti-task, designed to avoid work ... The infatuation with teams and the consequent requirement for individuals to work in meetings means that organisations are, quite simply, not getting the best performance from many of their members.

Amanda Sinclair,
Melbourne University Graduate School
of Management

Comes the revolution, and someone always get trampled. In Czarist Russia in 1917, it was Nicholas II and his family, along with the monied ruling class. In Cuba in 1959, it was the upper middle class, many of whom fled to Miami. In what was the modern-day Soviet Union, the stampede ran down the Communists, who were once fiery revolutionaries themselves but had softened into relics of a crumbling social and economic system.

It's not hard to predict a revolution's victims. Inevitably, they are those who held power under the old regime.

In revolutionary workplaces, those that are switching from Taylorism to teams, the victims are managers and supervisors. In their rush to empower self-managed teams as a path to greater efficiency and productivity, some organisations have disempowered managers and supervisors, and cut their numbers sharply.

Beverly Geber

Japan and Germany, the countries that are outperforming America in international trade, do not have less government or more motivated individuals. They are countries noted for their careful organisation of teams — teams that involve workers and managers, teams that involve suppliers and customers, teams that involve government and business.

There is nothing antithetical in American history, culture or traditions to teamwork. Teams were important in America's history — wagon trains conquered the West, men working together on the assembly line in American industry conquered the world, a successful national strategy and a lot of teamwork put an American on the moon first (and thus far, last). But American mythology extols only the individual — the Lone Ranger or Rambo. In America, halls of fame exist for almost every conceivable activity, but nowhere do Americans raise monuments in praise of teamwork. Only national mythology stands between Americans and the construction of successful economic teams. To say this is not, however, to say that change is easy. History is littered with the wrecks of countries whose mythologies were more important than reality.

Lester Thurow

If the United States is to compete effectively in the world in a way designed to enhance the real incomes of Americans, we must bring collective entrepreneurship to the forefront of the economy. That will require us to change our attitudes, to downplay the myth of the entrepreneurial hero, and to celebrate our creative teams.

First, we need to look for and promote new kinds of stories. In modern-day America, stories of collective entrepreneurship typically appear in the sports pages of the daily newspaper; time after time, in accounts of winning efforts we learn that the team with the best blend of talent won — the team that emphasised teamwork — not the team with the best individual athlete. The cultural challenge is to move these stories from the sports page to the business page.

Robert B. Reich

DECIDING AND SOLVING

COMMUNICATION SKILLS

METHODS OF GROUP DECISION-MAKING AND PROBLEM-SOLVING

The ways in which groups make decisions and solve problems lies at the very heart of understanding effectiveness in groups and teams. Are groups effective or ineffective at making decisions and solving problems? Do too many cooks spoil the broth, or do many hands make light work? Is it true that a camel is a horse designed by a committee?

TALKING POINTS

GROUP DECISION-MAKING? PROBLEM-SOLVING? OR BOTH?

People often toss around terms like 'decision-making' and 'problem-solving', but what do they really mean? Are they terms which can be used interchangeably? It's useful to treat them as separate but related concepts: let's presume here that 'decision-making' is a sub-set of the larger concept of 'problem-solving.' 'Problem-solving' is usefully seen as a sequence, such as:

1. Definition of a problem
2. Analysis of a problem
3. Generation of solutions
4. Prioritising or ranking of solutions
5. Execution or implementation
6. Evaluation.

'Decision-making' deals with steps 4 and 5 of this process.

We hear many complaints about the groups that we meet — committees, sub-committees, advisory groups, conferences, task forces, panels, or even the carload of friends deliberating on what kind of pizza to buy — but the fact remains that groups are part and parcel of living, and that they can be more or less effective according to our understanding of group processes. As more responsibility is passed to people working in teams, the need for this understanding becomes urgent.

What then are the strengths and weaknesses of group decision-making? Or, to put that another way, what are the weaknesses and strengths of individual decision-making and problem-solving? Table 6.1 gives a summary of the issues involved here. Let's how examine the pros and cons of the issue in greater detail.

Table 6.1: Pros and cons of group decision-making and problem-solving

Pro	Con
• can generate many new ideas	• not needed for routine decisions • individuals may generate more ideas
• can recall information accurately	• not always good at solving problems which require long chains of decisions and solutions
• can present multiplicity of roles (task, socio-emotional)	• destructive role-playing may crowd out benign task/socio-emotional role-playing
• can present wide range of skills, contributions, experiences, and styles of decision-making and problem-solving	• pressures towards homogeneity of styles, roles, skills, experiences and contributions are great — can produce Groupthink-type distortions
• authoritarian power can be checked	• minority tyranny can occur (dominant/authoritarian individual[s], cliques, factions, consensus holdouts) — hidden agendas • majority tyranny can occur — enforcement of conformity may stifle creative individuals, produce faulty decisions
• makes coordination easier	• coordination may become harder if group is riven with competition, empire-building
• decisions and solutions may be creative — synergy	• conservative, lowest-common denominator decisions may occur
• more competent risk management	• risky decisions may occur (risky shift, dilution of responsibility)
• motivation can increase through participation (quality/acceptance, mandate, input = output)	• group inertia may develop
• can bring about useful delays	• often slow and costly

(Source: Adapted from Eunson (1987), Koontz, O'Donnell and Weihrich (1980), Lee (1980), Hodgetts (1980), Stoner, Collins and Yetton (1985), Byrt (1980), Ferris and Wagner (1985), Burne (1993).)

Pro: many hands make light work

Thinking and remembering

Groups are good at generating new ideas (see table 6.1). They are also good at recalling information accurately. It would appear that the more minds there are present, the more ideas and memories can issue from them.

Deploying a multiplicity of roles

Groups can deploy a multiplicity of task and socio-emotional roles that an individual would be hard-pressed to match (so long as destructive roles do not overwhelm the 'good' roles, of course).

Deploying a multiplicity of skills, contributions, experiences, styles

Groups can make available a wide range of skills, contributions and experiences. They can also present a wide range of personality-based styles of decision-making and problem-solving, thus ensuring that blind spots, such as an individual might have, do not distort perceptions. Of course, groups can have blind spots too, particularly if the group is over-homogeneous and lacking in alternative points of view — too many 'birds of a feather flocking together'.

Blocking power players

The exercise of authoritarian power by individuals may become much harder when groups act as a countervailing power, providing a structure of checks and balances via committees and executives which 'lone rangers' will ignore at their peril. Even individuals within groups, such as dominant power-figures, may change their behaviour if they cannot simply bulldoze the group.

Making coordination easier

If all relevant decision-makers are present in a group, then obviously it can be much easier to coordinate operations. Any clashes, overlaps or bottlenecks can be made transparent, simply by the group sharing plans, and appropriate measures to forestall disaster can then be put into place.

Being creative

Decisions and solutions of groups can be more creative than those pro-duced by individuals if processes of synergy are taking place. Synergy means that the whole becomes greater than the sum of the parts. The sheer stimulus of others' ideas can produce creativity in some group members, particularly if the group has deliberately undertaken brain-storming or lateral thinking-type exercises in structured creativity.

Managing risk

Risks can sometimes be managed more competently within groups. A high-risk decision for an individual can often be a moderate-risk decision for a group because risk is a function of knowledge, and group deliber-ations may increase knowledge about a particular situation.

Increasing motivation

Motivation can be increased through participation. No matter how high the quality of a decision, it has to be accepted by those who are going to implement that decision. If people have not been consulted or involved in the decision-making process, there is no mandate for change, and people may either implement the decision in an apathetic fashion or may actively work against it — they don't own it, they are not stakeholders in it, so why should they try for it? Group involvement means group commitment. Group input means group output: more input, more output; less input, less output.

Creating useful delays

While groups are often criticised for being responsible for delays, as compared to individual processing of solutions and decisions, it is not often considered that delays might be a good thing. What if, for example, someone or some group decides that a problem could benefit from some benign neglect, or even better, suffer the death of a thousand sub-committees and attempts to get more data? This is not very honest, but such things do happen. This 'strength' of group decision-making and problem-solving also appears on the other side of table 6.1 as a weakness, but, as in many such things, it really depends upon your point of view (and your vested interest).

Con: too many cooks spoil the broth

The performance of groups — as compared to that of individuals — is less impressive in other areas. Sometimes it is better not to work in groups for the following reasons.

Not needed for making routine decisions/individuals may be better

Groups are not needed for routine decisions of most types: there is no need to agonise over which option to use when there is a standard operating procedure laid down and accepted by all. Also, it is by no means clear that groups are always better than individuals in generating numbers of new ideas: some research indicates that individuals can generate more new ideas than groups in certain circumstances.[1]

Not good at solving long-chain problems

Groups are not always so good at solving problems that require long chains of decisions and solutions. Thus groups are fine at playing concertos, but not composing them; or solving crossword puzzles but not writing them; or making films, but not writing novels.

Deploying destructive role-playing

Effective groups have an ideal combination of task and socio-emotional role-playing, with destructive role-playing kept to a minimum or perhaps even being non-existent. Ineffective groups — of which there are too many — allow destructive role-playing to become significant and even dominant.

Imposing homogeneity and conformity

Another mark of such all-too-common ineffective groups is that homogeneity of members' outlook is so high, it might as well be an individual — and, in fact, a broad-minded individual could easily be more effective than a narrow-minded group. And members of a group do not even have to be actually narrow-minded: they may be 'merely' submitting to pressure to conform to a narrow group norm, and as we have seen, such pressures can be enormous. In such situations, groups will not benefit from the potentially wide and deep range of skills, contributions, experiences and styles of decision-making and problem-solving present within its ranks, but will behave ineffectively, producing Groupthink-type distortions in its decisions and solutions.

Submitting to minority tyranny

Group members' personal needs for power and influence may overwhelm the collective good of the group. In addition to the formal agenda of the group, there may be one or several *hidden agendas* in operation with which individuals or sub-groups may try and manipulate others.

True group effectiveness occurs when the goals of individuals, groups and organisations (and societies) are in unison: this sublimely effective and enjoyable state of affairs does not occur as often as it should, and minority tyranny is a major reason for such failure.

Cliques or factions may dominate the group, and such cliques or factions may choose to paralyse and perhaps destroy the group rather than see their opponents win. Minority tyranny may occur when the group seeks consensus, and those who hold out from unanimity can block (horse-trade, compromise) with a power of leverage way beyond what their numbers would suggest. In fact, such a minority can be a minority of one — operating, of course, as an effective majority.

It may not be as subtle as holding out, of course: individuals may simply dominate groups because their power base is so overwhelming. Their power may be based on the ability to reward and punish, upon expertise, upon sheer force of personality or charisma, or because they just happen to be in the traditionally-deferred-to position of the boss — or a mixture of these. In these circumstances, the group is there to advise and consent only, or, even worse, to be a mere rubber stamp for the leader's wishes.

Submitting to majority tyranny

True majority tyranny can occur when sheer force of numbers swamps individuals or minorities. Such individuals may or may not be wrong, but unless other mechanisms operate (e.g., minority verdicts being published, or minorities defying group solidarity and leaking information to outsiders), we will never know. This enforcement of conformity can also lead to Groupthink-type situations.

Creating less, not more, coordination

Such intra-group squabbling, involving minorities or majorities, can also erode one of the potentially great strengths of groups, namely the ability to coordinate complex tasks. If the group is riven with competition and empire-building, the group's activities will become less coordinated than would be the case if, for example, one dominant individual with total power (and average or better-than-average competence) was running the same set of operations.

Being uncreative

Groups can, under good circumstances, produce high-quality, low-risk decisions and solutions. Circumstances, however, are not always good, and even when they are, a truly mediocre or truly disastrous group will produce low-quality, high-risk decisions and solutions. Majority tyranny, for example, can often lead to stodginess and conservatism, with groups producing lowest-common denominator decisions and solutions: the purity and strength of any original ideas entertained by the group have become diluted by endless compromises and gestures of appeasement towards powerful vested interests outside the group, and what the group finally comes up with ends up pleasing no-one and annoying many.

Creating too much risk

Alternatively, groups sometimes produce, not conservative decisions, but unstable radical decisions. Group decision-making and problem-solving is sometimes characterised by the *risky shift*, whereby groups make decisions that are riskier than those which would have been made by any of the group's members acting individually. While this is not always a bad thing, it can be bad, and indeed disastrous, if group members feel that group membership entails dilution of responsibility (what belongs to everyone belongs to no-one) and hence that normal procedures of risk evaluation are not relevant.

Succumbing to group inertia

Following on from such behaviour is the phenomenon of group inertia, wherein group members come to rely upon others to think and act for them. In such cases, an individual leader or an elite may emerge as the real force within the group, with the rest of the group acting as merely a rubber stamp, and thus being effectively redundant. ('When two people agree all the time, one of them is unnecessary.')

Creating too many delays

Groups can be slow and costly. Slowness is often related to group size: if group size increases arithmetically (1, 2, 3, 4 ...), then interactions between group members increase geometrically (1, 2, 4, 16 ...), and for everyone to talk to everyone else in a large group is time- and cash-consuming (avoidance or delay of action may, of course, be a deliberate strategy).

MAKING UP THE GROUP MIND

Most of the pros and cons we have just looked at relate to conventional, 'interacting' or 'normal' groups — the weekly meeting at work, the annual general meeting of the stamp collectors' association, or the group of friends sitting in a car who are trying to decide what restaurant to go to. We will look at approaches to making meetings of this Basic Interacting Group (BIG) more effective.

Alternatives to this BIG have been devised, usually in attempts to try and neutralise some of the factors listed on the Con side of our table (table 6.1). The full range of processes open to groups trying to make up their minds is:
1. Support of individual or leader
2. Voting
3. Consensus
4. Brainstorming
5. Delphi
6. Nominal Group Technique
7. Improved Nominal Group Technique.

Members of truly effective teams need to know about the strengths and weaknesses of all of these processes. Such strengths and weaknesses usually relate to the dynamics of communication within the team.

Let's have a look at all seven now.

1. Support of individual or leader

The processes of support, voting and consensus are visually summarised in figure 6.1.

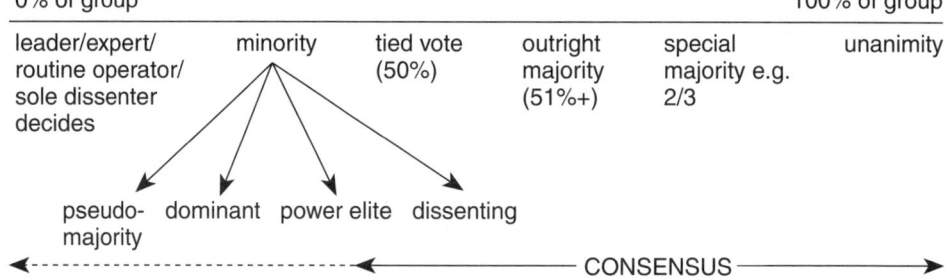

Figure 6.1: Some methods of reaching decisions and solutions in groups
(Source: Eunson (1987). Adapted with permission.)

What is it?

Support is concerned with the majority of the group deferring to one person. This one person might simply be an individual in a not-very-powerful position simply carrying out a routine procedure: so long as it is done competently, the rest of the group is happy to delegate authority and responsibility to that person to simply get on with the job.

A second situation in which the group might defer to an individual is when that individual does not have legitimate power — is not a 'boss' in the formal sense of the word — but instead has expert power: the individual is presumed to have special expertise in the area, and the group knows that it makes sense in terms of specialisation and division of labour to go along with what that individual wants to do.

Groups, of course, should not have blind faith in experts or even non-powerful individuals simply doing routine jobs — the potential for disaster is always present everywhere. But it makes sense for groups to simply monitor and support rather than act when individuals can act quite well by themselves.

The third type of support is that of support of leaders, or individuals with legitimate power — 'bosses'. This support comprises non-leaders witnessing the exercise of power, giving advice and consent to the leader, or even just being a mere rubber stamp. This process thus embodies a paradox: it comprises what is almost a non-role, and yet throughout most of recorded history, it has been the traditional role of the group. Were such decisions and solutions necessarily inferior to group-based ones? Not at all. Great leaders, and even some not-so-great ones, have done just fine throughout history exercising sole authority (keeping in mind, of course, that there was little basis for comparison with alternatives).

In modern organisations, such dynamics still exist — sometimes explicitly, sometimes implicitly. Sometimes the leader's power is so great that decisions and solutions are announced, and the group — an advisory panel, the totality of subordinates — has to like it or lump it. There is no participation; there are no teams; there is no industrial democracy. Sometimes the situation is more subtle, yet all the more insidious for that: the leader and the group mouth the rhetoric of participation, but the reality is that you'd better vote the right way, the 'consensus' you reach had better be the right one — or else.

The leader's real or perceived power needs to be high in such situations, and the leader needs to have a keen appreciation of the passive and active resistance and acceptance her/his decisions and solutions will meet with (for the heroic, and possibly for the paranoid leader, there is the comfort of the maxim 'one person in the right is a majority').

SUPPORT OF INDIVIDUAL OR LEADER: HOW TO DO IT

1. Group does nothing, or not much — individual in routine role or expert is given free rein. Group monitors and supports.
2. Group does nothing, or not much — listens to leader, advises, consents, supports — gives leader what s/he wants. Situation is either purely authoritarian, or mock-democratic.

What's good? What's bad?

Sometimes this approach leads to bad decisions and solutions, but sometimes to good ones. Irrespective of the quality of the leader's performance, it is often the case that such exercise of autocratic power profoundly demotivates others, and the entire story of organisational change in the twentieth century has been largely bound up with eroding such autocracy and strengthening democracy.

Yet the tension between the exercise of power by individuals and the exercise of power by groups remains an unresolved — and perhaps unresolvable — one. Certainly, while the move away from autocracy is to be applauded, sometimes inequality is not a disaster. Sometimes the input from the leader, or an individual expert, or a dominant extrovert is simply the best thing that is happening in a team, and asking them to 'hold back' in the interests of team participation may be seriously counter-productive.[2]

2. Voting

The Basic Interacting Group is the main arena for voting, although Brainstorming, Delphi and the Nominal Group approaches also use some form of voting.

What is it?

Voting can be either private (e.g., secret ballot) or public (e.g., show of hands). Groups choose one of these methods because they value public demonstration of belief over privacy, or privacy over public demonstration of belief, or because they simply haven't thought about the pros and cons of the method they use.

Voting in public

Public voting can be quick; it can be convenient in small groups; and it can force people to publicly commit themselves to a decision. It can, however, force people to conform to the pressure coming from articulate and assertive individuals who dismiss attempts to have secret ballots with remarks like: 'What have you got to hide?', and 'All right-thinking people know that there's only one way to vote on this one.'

Voting in private

Secret ballots have the virtue of protecting privacy and preventing pressure to conform in public settings, but they can be inconvenient in small groups, and they may allow people to vote in a particular way without demonstrating overt commitment to a belief, which may lead to hypocrisy (saying one thing, and voting for another). Electronic voting systems are now available for small groups, although some people still retain suspicions about the foolproofness of electronic voting.

Various constellations of minorities and majorities are revealed by voting patterns.

Veto

A veto is the right exercised by an individual or a representative of a group to reject or forbid something. It is a super-vote, the presence of which stops an entire process of decision-making; effectively, it is a minority of one acting as a majority. Sometimes the veto is an official one, e.g., the vote of a chief executive officer, who has powers of veto under the standing orders of the board of directors; sometimes it is an unofficial one, e.g., the vote of a person who wields so much power and/ or expertise that his/her opinion is ignored by the group at its peril.

Pseudo-majority

A pseudo-majority can exist when a minority exercises power via inequalities in votes. A political party exercising a gerrymander, or stockholders in a company having different classes of stocks and voting rights, or a minority using proxy votes of people outside the group currently meeting — all use this approach.

Dominant minority

A dominant minority is one which rules when its opponents cannot agree enough to form a majority: for example, if group A with 30 per cent of power and group B with 30 per cent of power loathe each other so much that they cannot form a coalition, then group C, with 40 per cent, effectively controls the wider group.

Power elite

A power elite may control the group in much the same way as a strong individual leader does, either officially or unofficially. An elite may make decisions and not be challenged by others, or may influence or control the votes of others.

Dissenting minority

A dissenting minority occurs in many groups, for example, a panel or bench of judges: the majority may give a verdict or decision, but a minority of one or several judges may, rather than remain silent or give the impression of unanimity, issue a statement of dissent.

Tied votes

Tied votes occur when two sub-groups each have 50 per cent of power (of course, tied votes could occur just as well where we might have three sub-groups each with $33\frac{1}{3}$ per cent, etc.). Groups sometimes have mechanisms for resolving such ties — for example, the chair has the casting vote, or tied votes on a motion mean that the motion is lost, or the casting vote is drawn from a hat.

Straight majorities

These are usually anything over 50 per cent. Some straight majorities are in fact pseudo-unanimous: government ministries or cabinets usually operate on the principle of cabinet solidarity, i.e., decisions made by straight majority (or perhaps by a powerful leader or power elite) must be defended by all ministers in public, with (officially) no breaches attributable to dissenting minorities or 'leakers'.

In the democratic tradition, the majority is always right: *vox populi, vox Dei*: the voice of the people is the voice of God. There are, however, many who doubt this, arguing that quantity cannot substitute for quality (for example, in Hendrik Ibsen's play, *An Enemy of the People*, the hero Stockmann argues that the majority is always wrong: majorities, by definition, says Stockmann, are mediocre and conservative, and cannot discern current realities and future trends as well as perceptive individuals and elites can).

Special majorities

Special majorities are often required on extremely important decisions — for example, two-thirds majority rather than simply 50 per cent.

Unanimity

Unanimity, or 100 per cent agreement, is unusual, but is sometimes required for decisions. In some parts of the world, a unanimous verdict is required of juries in trials for crimes such as murder, while in other parts of the world, a straight or special majority is required. The group dynamics of juries changes considerably according to what type of majority verdict is required. A single individual blocking a unanimous decision can have as much power as a consensus holdout (see Consensus, below) or a leader with veto.

VOTING : HOW TO DO IT

1. Pre-determine what particular type of voting chosen needs to achieve: anonymity of voters? public demonstration of belief? speed/convenience? clear/unambiguous mandate for important decisions? preservation of reserve power of chief executive?
2. Establish rules, conventions, e.g., a tied vote will be lost.
3. Arrange for special resources, e.g., ballot papers, tally sheets, whiteboards, electronic voting equipment.
4. Vote.

What's good? What's bad?

Voting, in all its various forms, is possibly as old as giving support to an individual or leader as a group process. It can provide a clear quantitative view of what people's opinions really are. With public display voting, accountability is possible, unlike the situation with secret ballots in BIGs and the various nominal groups, and unlike the situation in the public 'voting' in Brainstorming and Consensus (where, in worst-case situations, it is possible to mumble assent and no-one is the wiser as to where you really stand). Private voting, nevertheless, preserves anonymity and thus neutralises the potentially oppressive dynamics of personality and status in groups.

It is public voting — a show of hands, for example — that presents problems for many people. It can induce conformity because of group pressure. It takes a lot of courage to be in a minority, or even to be a minority of one. Also, voting can encourage a win–lose mentality, which can be divisive in a group.

3. Consensus

What is it?

Consensus is a method of reaching agreement without taking a vote. Some response from all group members is required, of course, either positive or negative and either verbal or non-verbal. The pros and cons of issues are thrashed out at length, with someone such as the chair or a facilitator trying to find common areas of agreement between disputing parties. Consultant Edgar Schein has said that elimination of dissent may not be the aim of consensus: a consensus decision is reached when a dissenting group member can say:

I understand what most of you would like to do. I personally would not do that, but I feel that you understand what my alternative would be. I have had sufficient opportunity to sway you to my point of view, but clearly have not been able to do so. Therefore I will gladly go along with what most of you wish to do.[3]

While consensus is not always the ideal tool for teams to use,[4] it is particularly useful where all team members need to be committed to the decision or solution in order to implement it.

CONSENSUS: HOW TO DO IT

1. Appoint a leader.
2. Leader announces that decision will not be reached by voting/; instead, she/he will periodically test for consensus by asking: 'Can you support this decision?'

    Members will respond verbally.

    Members need to consider whether they are at the point of minimal agreement, where they can say: 'I understand what most of you would like to do. I personally would not do that, but I feel that you understand what my alternative would be. I have had sufficient opportunity to sway you to my point of view, but clearly have not been able to do so. Therefore I will gladly go along with what most of you wish to do.'
3. Avoid bargaining ('I'll vote for this if you vote for that.').
4. Avoid abdicating/giving in/changing minds merely to reach agreement and reduce conflict.
5. Avoid chance mechanisms (e.g., flipping a coin).
6. Encourage expressions of differences of opinions: see differences as chances to generate more options for group, not causes of conflict.
7. Encourage participation of all: listen, observe non-verbal reactions.
8. Avoid a win-lose mentality; strive for win-win solutions.
9. Don't expect a quick fix — this is a time-intensive process.

What's good? What's bad?

Consensus has recently gained importance as a method of making decisions and producing solutions within groups and teams. Consensus is used in Japanese Quality Circles, for instance: Quality Circles, or QCs, are groups of workers and managers who seek to maintain and improve the quality of goods such as automobiles or videotape recorders. The spectacular improvements in the quality of Japanese manufactured goods from the 1960s onwards is sometimes attributed largely to the extreme effectiveness of QCs and the consensus method. Other effects of the process, such as improved motivation and job satisfaction, have also been observed. Attempts — some successful, some not so successful — have been made to implement QC-type work organisation in Western countries. Successful Western QCs have, using consensus methods, achieved similar improvements in quality, motivation and job satisfaction.

Further, although consensus is time-consuming as opposed to other methods of making decisions and solving problems, it may be that if all meeting participants feel as though they 'own' the decision or solution, they will probably be more committed to implementing it. This may well save time in the long run, minimising misunderstandings and also minimising hostility (and perhaps even undermining and obstruction) from such participants who feel as though they are the losers in a win/lose situation.

Some have criticised the method of consensus, suggesting that cultures such as the Japanese are very group- and cooperation-oriented, whereas Western cultures are more individual- and competition-oriented, and that Japanese 'cooperation' may, in fact, simply be conformity by members of the groups and manipulation of the groups by paternalistic managements.[5] This is not to say that Westerners cannot learn to be more cooperative: in fact, some writers such as Lester Thurow have pointed out that European nations such as Germany have a strong group-oriented tradition quite separate from that of Japan's, and unless nations such as America adapt such a group ethos, they are destined for the historical scrap-heap.[6] Clearly then, consensus is not simply a small-scale process that occurs in groups and has no wider repercussions: it, and the other methods of group decision-making and problem-solving we are analysing here, may have national, cultural and historical dimensions to them.

Consensus, even though an effective tool in some situations, can, however, go wrong in a number of ways:[7]

(a) It can be used by manipulative chairmen and/or lazy group members to lower, rather than increase participation ('We all agree on this, don't we?' — nods, mumbles).

(b) It may become the paramount goal, causing people to suppress their opposition or to say they agree when they honestly do not.

(c) It is frustrating to all members to have to keep discussing a subject long after their minds are made up, simply because they are hoping to convince honest dissenters (a waste of time and an embarrassment to the dissenters).

(d) It permits one dissenter to make the decision for the whole group, which destroys the basic purpose for which the group was convened.

(e) It can distort and mask normal patterns of conflict and power, giving a false impression of harmony.

4. Brainstorming

What is it?

Brainstorming is a way of trying to break the dynamics (or more accurately, the statics) of groups that are conformist, that have become stuck in a rut of logical, analytical thinking and that cannot make the jump to imaginative, creative thinking.

Creativity cannot be programmed or commanded: it usually happens only when group members can step outside their task roles and relax and have fun. This does not normally happen in work- or task-oriented situations. So much of what we do is concerned with making sure that existing processes are operating, and that like things and ideas are tidily pigeon-holed together; yet so much creativity is about the relating of things and ideas that were previously *unrelated*.[8]

Brainstorming as a process depends upon two principles:

(a) Defer judgement

(b) Quantity breeds quality.

Normally, we judge our own and others' ideas immediately they see the light of day. This, suggested Brainstorming's inventor, Alex Osburn, is often a bad thing, in that many good ideas strike people as being too way-out or impractical, when in fact they may be simply ahead of their time. How 'practical' would aeroplanes or automobiles have been to a citizen of the eighteenth, or even very early twentieth, century? Quantity can breed quality, Osburn argued, if an enormous amount of dud ideas nevertheless contained one good idea.[9]

BRAINSTORMING: HOW TO DO IT

1. Select one problem that is specific, and where novel and multiple solutions are possible.
2. Select a Brainstorming group. Limit group size to six to twelve members.
3. Try to have participants who are of roughly equal status (the presence of superiors and subordinates tends to freeze up creativity).
4. Inform the group of the problem several days before the session.
5. Appoint a leader/facilitator, and a secretary who records all suggestions.
6. Try to heighten stimuli, and thus disinhibit members: e.g., super-enthusiastic encouragement from leader, bright lighting, music.
7. Exhort members to come up with as many far-out solutions as possible.
8. Encourage building on other people's ideas (hitch-hiking, piggy-backing, cross-fertilising).
9. Brainstorm for 30–45 minutes.
10. Appoint an evaluation group of 3–5 (odd number to avoid tied votes). Evaluation group members may be drawn from the Brainstorming group, or from outside it.
11. Organise solutions into categories. Assign priorities, based upon practicality. Vary or delete steps according to need.

What's good? What's bad?

Solutions emerging from brainstorming are often zany and impractical, but occasionally illuminating — and, after all, that is what the process is meant to achieve. Brainstorming, however, should be used only where problems can be stated specifically, where there is a possibility of multiple solutions, and where the solution or concept or thing being sought is genuinely new.

Group cohesiveness can be built into brainstorming, especially when extroverts can give full play to their sense of play and desire to outdazzle peers with ideas which are more and more way out.[10] Brainstorming has been criticised, however, because of a number of apparent weaknesses:

(a) Its usefulness is limited to relatively simple problems.

(b) Creativity can collapse into anarchy.

(c) Dominant individuals can have too much influence.

(d) It is often inferior to nominal groups or individuals working alone in terms of output of creative ideas.[11]

5. Delphi

What is it?

The group decision-making/problem-solving technique called Delphi was first used in America in the 1950s to predict the impacts of Russian bomb attacks on US industry. It was named after the Greek town of Delphi where, in ancient times, priests called upon the god Apollo to give them insight into the future. The technique basically consists of administering a series of questionnaires to a panel of experts, asking them to predict probabilities of certain events. The experts are all in different geographical locations, do not meet, and have no direct or written communication with one another. Various rounds of questionnaires are used to refine the predictions. It is thus a method of constructing consensus at a distance.

Delphi has been used in various areas, such as military, educational, marketing and local government planning.

What's good? What's bad?

Delphi can remove the potentially harmful group pressure to conform that is present in Brainstorming and Basic Interacting Groups. Anonymous experts are free to make up their own minds in a quiet, reflective environment, and each participant has an equal opportunity to contribute, with all ideas being given equal consideration. A large quantity of ideas can be generated, and some precision can be given. ('What is the probability of X happening in the next six years?')

Delphi is also useful when it is impractical to bring together people who are widely separated by geography. The revolution in data transfer in the past few years now means that experts being sampled in the Delphi process can use computers to electronically receive, complete and return questionnaires. They can interact in 'real time' as they would in a face-to-face encounter. However, Delphi can lead to perhaps too much detachment on the part of the participants. Because others are not close at hand to clarify their ideas or terms, confusion can arise. Any conflicts in predictions of the future are 'solved' by simple majority vote, which may mean that the correct prediction will be swamped.

Related to this, Delphi panels are usually made up of experts in a given field, who may be too close to the problem, or more bluntly, just plain wrong (indeed, experts may be part of the problem rather than the solution).[11]

The apparent precision of the 'predictions' ('Of the panel, 54 per cent think that this has an 86 per cent chance of happening.') may trick people into half-believing that the future can be predicted scientifically.

Finally, Delphi is very time-consuming: a three-round process may take over 45 days to complete, which presupposes very high levels of organisation on the part of the organisers and very high levels of motivation on the part of the participants, although some of these problems are reduced using computer networking.

DELPHI: HOW TO DO IT

1. Select a problem, or problems. Usually, these relate to possible future events, where it is meaningful to give a quantitative probability as to the likelihood (or unlikelihood) of such events ever occurring.
2. Devise first round questionnaire. Items should relate to estimating probabilities of events A, B, C.
3. Select a panel of experts. Such experts should preferably be geographically separate from each other, preferably unknown to each other, and not in communication with each other.
4. Send out questionnaires.
5. Collect questionnaires.
6. Analyse questionnaires for trends, convergences, patterns.
7. Devise next round questionnaire. Items should now be more specific, asking for estimates of probabilities of events based upon trends, convergences and patterns observed in first round responses.
8. Repeat steps 4–7 until sufficient trends are clear enough upon which to base forecasts.

---

6. Nominal group technique (NGT)

What is it?

Like Delphi, NGT can be used when normal group dynamics of conformity and pressure might possibly distort decision-making and problem-solving in groups. As with Delphi, NGT involves individuals making written responses to problems, but like brainstorming and interacting groups, there is some group discussion. However, in some parts of the process, the members might as well be separate individuals in different places: hence the group is 'nominal', or a group in name only.

NOMINAL GROUP TECHNIQUE: HOW TO DO IT

1. Select a problem.
2. Select a group of five to nine people.
3. Convene the meeting in a normal venue. Appoint a leader.
4. The leader puts the problem to the group.
5. Writing phase (10–20 minutes): group members begin, silently and individually, to write out possible solutions to the problem.
6. Idea recording phase (5–10 minutes): leader asks each member in turn to give an idea, recording these on a chart or board. Leader continues to ask for further contributions from members, keeping to the original sequence ('round-robin reporting') until all ideas have been recorded.

   No discussion at this stage. All ideas are numbered.
7. Discussion phase (10–30 minutes): all ideas are clarified and discussed, but not to the stage where passionate differences are allowed to emerge.
8. Voting stage (10–30 minutes): each individual member selects a number of ideas as being better than the rest, ranking each idea according to a weighting system (e.g., 5 = excellent, 1 = just all right).

   These votes are written on cards, with the idea number at top right and ranking number at bottom right (usually underlined, or circled, or in another colour, or with 'R' beside it, to ensure no confusion with idea number occurs). The leader collects these cards, shuffles them (to preserve anonymity), and then records the votes for the various ideas.
9. If no clear preferences emerge, continue discussion and hold a second ballot.

What's good? What's bad?

Nominal Group Technique relieves individuals of pressures to conform, allowing individuality to emerge: there is less pressure than in BIGs or Brainstorming groups from other group members who might be more articulate or of higher or lower status. Because there is more anonymity in the process, attention can be switched away from personalities to the ideas themselves. This is not to say that the group is exclusively task-role oriented, as often happens in Delphi, for example: the discussion period or periods allows socio-emotional-role orientation, as well. NGT groups often produce a lot of ideas, and the outcome of the group — expressed as quantified priorities — is often much clearer than in BIGs.

NGT of course has its drawbacks, such as:

(a) It can only be used to solve one problem at a time.
(b) True anonymity cannot be guaranteed because of verbal 'inputting'.

(c) Spontaneity and freewheeling enthusiasm can be inhibited.

(d) It requires a skilled leader.

(e) Group size must be small (nine or fewer), otherwise it takes too long.

(f) It sometimes makes people uncomfortable because of its controlled or ritualistic sequencing.

7. Improved nominal group technique (INGT)

What is it?

INGT is similar to NGT, as the names would suggest, except that ideas are 'inputted' prior to the meeting. Participants write on cards and submit them. The cards are analysed to see if the meeting might be improved by bringing along other people or specialised resources.[12]

IMPROVED NOMINAL GROUP TECHNIQUE: HOW TO DO IT

1. Select a problem to be solved.

2. Announce meeting time, venue. Distribute multiple copies of blank cards to members beforehand. Ask members to write down one solution per card. Members should not identify themselves on the cards. Specify a deadline, say three days before meeting, when cards must be submitted. Allow for anonymous submission, e.g., a drop-in or suggestion box.

3. Collect cards. Analyse to see if a meeting would benefit by bringing along other people or specialised resources. Arrange these if needed.

4. Publish list of ideas before the meeting. Number and list — do not change in any way. Provide more cards in case this list stimulates further ideas; members may bring these along to meeting and submit anonymously.

5. Hold meeting. Leader asks for submission of further cards. Anonymity is maintained via members with no new ideas submitting blank cards.

6. Continue with normal Nominal Group Technique procedure of discussion and voting.

What's good? What's bad?

INGT allows true anonymity in the idea generation phase as well as the voting phase. Any inhibitions on the basis of personality and status experienced by members should be thus non-existent. Meeting times can be reduced, because many or all ideas would be already known and would have been transcribed onto a board or flip chart before the meeting. Because the bottleneck of one-person-per-turn transcribing of ideas is reduced or eliminated, it is more practical to run bigger meetings if necessary. Also, the leader and the people doing the transcribing/ recording can have creative input, at least in the idea generation before the meeting. This is in contrast to their neutral role in other group settings like NGT (and Brainstorming and Consensus).

On the down side, INGT shares some of the drawbacks of NGT — it requires a skilled leader, it can only be used to process one idea at a time, it can inhibit spontaneity, and participants might feel uncomfortable with the 'artifical' dynamics of the process.

We've now looked at seven methods used by groups in making up their minds — or having them made up for them. The pros and cons of the various methods are listed in table 6.2.

Table 6.2: Pros and cons of seven methods of group problem-solving and decision-making

Method	Pro	Con
1. Support of individual or leader	• individual in routine role or expert can get on with job • leader can act quickly • leader may produce good solutions and decisions	• individuals doing routine tasks and experts can be wrong • leader may miss vital perceptions, opinions, information • followers may become demotivated and hostile or apathetic
2. Voting	• can provide a clear, quantitative view of opinions • can preserve anonymity, and thus neutralise negative group pressures • can ensure accountability	• can lead to negative group pressure • can lead to hypocrisy, lack of accountability • can lead to win/lose mentality
3. Consensus	• can avoid win/lose mentality • can build commitment to decisions and solutions • can lead to improvements in product quality, motivation, job satisfaction	• can reduce participation • can cause delays • holdouts can effectively decide for whole group • may mask conflict and power dynamics
4. Brainstorming	• many ideas generated — often quantity does mean quality • group cohesiveness can be built • extroverts' energy can be harnessed to group's purpose • premature judging/closure avoided • fun, zaniness, creativity given legitimate role (socio-emotional needs satisfied)	• usefulness limited to relatively simple problems • creativity can collapse into anarchy • dominant individuals can have too much influence • often inferior to NGT or individuals working alone in producing solutions

Method	Pro	Con
5. Delphi	• removes group pressures to conform • all ideas given equal consideration • anonymity allows group to focus on issues rather than personalities • large quantity of ideas generated • ideas can be quantified easily • useful even when/especially when group is geographically dispersed • task needs satisfied	• participants can become overly detached — 'too much' task orientation • confusion can arise because clarification is difficult (less so in real-time Delphi) • conflicts are 'solved' by brute force of majority vote • experts are not always right • apparent precision of predictions may be spurious • time consuming (less so with real-time Delphi) • requires lots of organisation • requires high level of motivation of participants
6. Nominal group technique	• removes group pressure to conform • all ideas given equal consideration • anonymity allows group to focus on issues rather than on personalities • task — and socio-emotional needs satisfied • many ideas generated • voting, priorities give precise basis for decision-making and problem-solving	• can only be used for one problem at a time • can inhibit spontaneity, freewheeling, enthusiasm • can make people uncomfortable because of degree of control required • requires a skilled leader • true anonymity not guaranteed • suitable only for small groups
7. Improved nominal group technique	• guarantees anonymity • allows for provision of special resources, other people • can shorten meetings • allows leader, recorders to participate creatively • suitable for large groups	• can only be used for one problem at a time • can inhibit spontaneity, freewheeling, creativity • can make people uncomfortable because of degree of control required • requires a skilled leader

(Source: Adapted from Delbecq, Van der Ven and Gustafson (1975), Davis (1981), Eunson (1987), Fox (1989), Van Gundy (1990).)

All of these techniques have much to offer. All of them can be used to resolve conflict in teams and all of them, with the possible exception of Delphi, can be used to substantially improve the effectiveness of meetings — the arena in which much conflict takes place. Let's now consider meetings and conflict resolution in greater detail.

7

MEETING AND RESOLVING

COMMUNICATION SKILLS

We now know a fair amount about group processes — about the dynamics of dominance and submission (and how to minimise such dynamics), about creative and routine processes, about the use of emotion and opinion versus fact, about the complementary channel or dimension of non-verbal communication. Let's apply these now, and look at two major areas of concern for teams — meetings, and the resolution of conflict. There is some overlap between these two areas, particularly when conflict occurs within meetings.

MEETINGS: THE TEAM IN ACTION

The meeting is the key arena in which team members interact. Meetings, however, have had a bad press — 'a place where minutes are kept and hours lost' is one of the more charitable descriptions. Yet it doesn't have to be that way. We have picked up a few insights into groups and teams along the way in this book — let's apply them now to come up with some strategies for truly effective meetings. Table 7.1 lists such strategies.

Table 7.1: Strategies for effective meetings[1]

Strategy	Details
1. Ask is this meeting really necessary?	Are you having a meeting because you always have a meeting at this time? What would happen if you didn't? Try not having the meeting for one day, or week, or month, and see what happens. Do you need a meeting to communicate, when, in fact, you really only require a memo, teleconference, one-on-one meeting or bulletin-board notice?
2. Decide on objectives of meeting in advance.	Discuss with participants what should/should not be talked about, and structure the agenda accordingly. Plan. If planning is not possible, if crisis meetings have to be called, that's okay — but if more than two crisis meetings have to be called in a week, then the group needs to have a meeting to discuss this very fact: are panic merchants, adrenalin junkies and 'meetingaholics' in charge, or is the whole organisation in crisis, and therefore in need of strategic change, rather than the mere tactical manoeuvring that meetings can supply?

Strategy	Details
3. Ensure agendas are clear.	Agendas should give headline and background information. If participants are required to bring materials, stipulate that fact or attach a list to the agenda. Proposers of items might be requested to append outlines of two solutions to the problem. This discourages frivolity, helps torpedo Groupthink and encourages pre-digestion of facts and values.
4. Time-limit agenda items.	This helps spike Parkinson's Fifth Law: the amount of time spent on any agenda item is in inverse proportion to its importance.
5. Be ready to abandon agenda if necessary.	Agendas are servants, not masters. A well-thought-out agenda is a powerful tool for chanelling creativity and conflict, but if matters arise that need instant consideration, be ready to abandon or defer agenda items.
6. Remember the rule of halves.	Get all items to be discussed at the meeting to the agenda maker at the half-way point between meetings (e.g., in the second week of a four-week cycle).
7. Remember the rule of three-quarters.	At the three-quarter point between meetings, all relevant material should be sent to group members.
8. Remember the rule of thirds.	Schedule the heavy items for the middle third of the meeting: this is when people are most fresh and concentrated, and latecomers are present as are early-goers. (Most meetings usually end up considering the most important items last, with maximum time pressure and maximum irritation apparent, and people voting more with their feet than their hands.)
9. Invite the right people.	Invite participants selectively — too many will lead to people being bored, while too few will lead to 'nobody told us' troubles. Four to seven people is ideal — twelve is the outside limit.
10. Select a good chairperson.	A good chairperson is someone who is happy to know where he/she is, happy to feel significant, and happy to be in a position where strong convictions are not needed. If a chairperson has strong opinions on an issue, establish a norm — make it routine — for that person to vacate the chair in favour of someone else while speaking on the issue. Don't confuse roles of referee and combatant. If the chair is also the power figure — the boss — and he or she really wants good quality decision-making, as opposed to sycophancy and resentment, then he/she should send out signals that all views will be given equal time and consideration, and that the group is not a rubber-stamp mechanism (e.g., the chairperson doesn't express opinions explicitly or implicitly [non-verbally]) until others have). See next point.
11. Clarify decision-making and problem-solving procedures.	Is this a democracy, or something else? Total, mock or modified democracies can make good decisions, but it should be spelt out just what the procedures are. Are decisions made by vote (show of hands, secret ballot), by one person, consensus, or other means? It's very useful to establish a norm that techniques such as the nominal group ones can be brought in merely because one individual requests it. Even repressive despots should be able to see that nominal group approaches can help out in generating alternatives for problem-solving, as distinct from being used in decision-making by secret ballot. The deferral of judgement inherent in brainstorming, or the sampling of opinion from distant experts inherent in Delphi, are also strategies that should be seen as normal.

(continued)

Table 7.1: Strategies for effective meetings (*continued*)

Strategy	Details
12. Start on time.	Don't punish the virtuous and reward the sinful by delaying the start. Get serious about time management.
13. Finish on time.	Meetings usually drag on because of the 'death of the meeting' phase — people get comfy, and don't want to go home.
14. Be aware of, and respect, motives.	People have different motives for attending meetings. As Winston Fletcher remarks, we go to meetings because: • we feel lonely working on our own • we are scared of decisions being taken in our absence • it makes us feel important • we want a rest from our real work • we want to offload the responsibility for a difficult decision • we particularly like the sound of our own voices • simply because the meeting happens to be happening Oh yes, of course — and to work.[2]
15. Don't avoid conflict.	Don't avoid it inside the meeting because you won't be able to avoid it outside if you do — and it won't be on your terms or your ground. Conflict is normal. (Note conflict resolution strategies, p. 120.)
16. Get emotions and opinions out in the open.	These are not luxuries, and the cost of suppression is too high. Don't be deluded by facts — facts can be arranged and edited to suit any opinion. As to emotions, remember the next point.
17. Use assertive feedback.	Establish the norm of people using the assertive feedback sequence. (When you … this happens … and I feel … would you … because … I would feel … what do you think?')
18. Use active listening and questioning.	Ensure that no-one plays non-listening games and that questioning techniques are appropriate.
19. Be sensitive to non-verbal communication.	Watch for signs of boredom (doodling, wandering eyes, yawning, fidgeting, slumped bodies, glazed expressions, sleep); ascertain whether the problem lies with the speaker or the listener(s), and take appropriate action. Watch for signs of frustration and/or disagreement (shaking of heads, pursing of lips, tapping of pens, picking of imaginary lint off clothes, scratching of heads, doodling violently, rolling of eyes, raising of eyebrows, conspiratorial winking, looking at watches, facial expressions of despair, sighing) and seek verbal translations: your purpose is not to embarrass, but to make it easier for people to speak — so don't mention the body language signs, merely ask questions such as 'Would you like to jump in here, James, and give us your view?'
20. Optimise role-playing and individual differences.	Try and achieve the most synergistic blend of socio-emotional and task role-playing, and assertively defuse destructive role-playing. Try for synergy again with individual personality differences: don't use psychological name-calling and pigeon-holing, but — where appropriate — point out that differences of opinion may be more down to style than substance, and that each style is valid.

Strategy	Details
21. **Establish norms of trust and openness.**	Attempt, wherever possible, to minimise or eliminate politicking, game-playing and hidden agendas.
22. **Avoid Groupthink and Abilene Paradox.**	Set up and rotate the role of devil's advocate — someone who is given permission by the group to present, without recriminations or pressure to conform, the most wrong-headed, bloody-minded, nit-picking alternative viewpoints. Establish a norm of assertive confrontation.
23. **Control speakers.**	Do this by nominating two or three speakers at a time, in sequence: this minimises ego-tripping and top-of-the-heading (if that is your aim), and maximises succinctness because of speakers' guilt about others in the queue.
24. **Control the strong; protect the weak.**	Garrulous extroverts are not always simply empty vessels — they are often strong on both quantity and quality of ideas. Nevertheless, they can't have all the airtime, and it may be necessary to have them stick to the agenda, or put their ideas in writing for next time, or chair a sub-committee on the issue. Draw out the silent: some may be useless, but some may have the meaning of life. If you're confident that it won't be too divisive, it is sometimes useful to have a meeting's proceedings taken down word for word in shorthand (perhaps secretly), transcribed, counted for words per person, and the data transferred to a pie chart to be presented at the next meeting.
25. **Leave the heavies until last.**	Establish a norm that the most senior and/or high status people — which may include the chair and/or boss — don't talk until the more junior members have spoken. This doesn't always work, but it can help the more inhibited have their say. Heavies should cooperate — their egos can be stroked by having the last word.
26. **Use the meeting as a feedback, control and reinforcement tool.**	Make the meeting the forum for presentations, progress reports, documentation of the process and products of the team's work, and general sharing of feedback. Keep the team on track by monitoring and proactively sensing out potential disasters and opportunities; breakdowns in communications; overlaps; members stepping on each other's toes; putting each other's noses out of joint; customers and clients getting angry and frustrated; and so forth. When things go wrong, share the upset, avoid witch-hunts, analyse and learn. When things go right, celebrate together, and give credit where it's due.
27. **Use gimmicks.**	To motivate people to finish quickly and work efficiently, try tactics such as holding stand-up meetings, and scheduling meetings immediately prior to lunch or knock-off time.
28. **End with a call to action; write it all down.**	Ensure that concrete action comes out of the meeting, that people have a sense of achievement. Keep a record of who agreed to do what, where, when, by when, how, and with or on whom. Reproduce and distribute as minutes (with an 'Action' column), and make this the basis for the next agenda.

(Source: adapted with permission from Eunson (1987).)

RESOLVING CONFLICT IN TEAMS

The meeting is obviously a crucial arena wherein conflicts develop and are — sometimes — resolved. The impetus for solution may, however, have to come from outside the team if there are not the resources, will or power within the team to effect such an outcome. Table 7.2 lists some strategies that may prove of use in resolving conflict within teams. Most of these strategies can also be used for resolving conflict between a team and the outside world of the organisation — generally or more specifically, other competing teams.

Table 7.2: Strategies for managing conflict[3]

Strategy	Details
1. Check non-verbal communications.	Watch non-verbal behaviour; it's an early warning sign of conflict (as well as more positive situations). Catch conflict when it is merely annoyance rather than blundering on to rage. Ask people to verbalise their feelings.
2. Check stages.	Sometimes conflict is predictable because that is what happens at one particular stage of group development (Forming/Storming/Norming/Performing — see p. 125). That doesn't make it any less real, but it suggests hope via the establishment of new norms. Be careful — no-one likes to be told that they're 'just going through a phase — what you feel is not real, or if real, trivial'.
3. Invoke a common enemy.	Throughout history, warring tribes have only been brought together when confronted with a common enemy. Does one exist? If not, can one — or the illusion of one — be created?
4. Create superordinate goals.	A superordinate goal is one that can only be achieved by the combined efforts of all parties. Identify one or create one.
5. Appoint a common superior.	A superior common to one or several teams can act as a disinterested adjudicator between squabbling factions, or else as a 'knocker-together-of-heads', who orders sub-groups/factions/cliques and groups to bury their differences or else be buried themselves (metaphorically, of course).
6. Use bargaining.	Sub-groups or groups may enter into bargaining or negotiation ('We'll do this for you if you do that for us') whenever mutually advantageous.
7. Try combinations.	Sub-groups or groups may enter into a coalition for the duration of a crisis. They may merge, or may be forced to merge.
8. Use proximity.	Sub-groups or groups may be forced to work together. The hope, sometimes realised, sometimes forlorn, is that interpersonal proximity will turn suspicion into grudging respect, and then liking. Rotating staff between groups is also based on such hopes, as is holding combined social functions.
9. Use planning.	Planning techniques, such as the critical path method, provide an authoritative and neutral way of sequencing tasks to be performed by different sub-groups or groups, thus reducing potential for conflict.

Strategy	Details
10. Put skills training into practice.	Training in the type of skills we have been considering earlier — listening, feedback, seeking consensus — may help warring sub-groups and groups to shift their attention away from content matters to process matters.
11. Use mediation.	A third party can be brought in to help examine content and process issues when conflict arises. Role clarification can be of use here.
12. Create more resources.	Conflicts are often about scarce resources. If possible, create new ones. If not possible, try cosmetic solutions, like giving honorific names to fairly humble tasks and positions.
13. Go cool.	Emotionally disengage from the team or organisation. After all, it's not family and friends — does it really matter?
14. Go.	Walk away, if you can. Transfer elsewhere, temporarily or permanently, take a holiday, or resign.

(Source: Adapted with permission from Eunson (1990).)

QUESTIONS, QUESTIONS ...

1. Consider the last two meetings you have attended. How many rules were broken? How many were observed? What can be done to improve the observed: broken ratio?
2. What other strategies might there be for effective meetings?
3. Think of two conflicts in which you are currently involved. What strategies might be most effective in resolving them? Why?
4. What other strategies might there be for resolving conflict?

THE WORLD BEYOND THE TEAM
COMMUNICATION SKILLS

REPRESENTING THE TEAM EFFECTIVELY

You have been asked to do a presentation on how the team is going. What will you do? Up until now, we have been concentrating upon communication processes and skills inside the team. Now the focus shifts outwards. (See figure 1.1, p. 2.) Nevertheless, all of the processes and skills that serve well inside the team form the foundation for the processes and skills you need to know about when operating outside the team, or at least, when operating away from your home base — the entire team, or a large fraction of it, may be doing the communicating along with you.

Of course, representing your team can happen in more routine situations. You might be walking down a corridor, or having lunch, when someone from outside the team asks a general question, such as: 'So how's it all going?' Your response will be an accurate reflection of how you feel about the team. If things are going well, you will give a positive response. If things aren't going so well, then you will have to work out how loyal you need to be to the team, and also how truthful you will need to be. Many of the communication skills appropriate to more formal situations will be brought into play. If things aren't too bad, accentuate the positive, and don't air the team's dirty washing to people who may not care or may, in fact, use it against you. If you find that your loyalty is somewhat problematic, and this is becoming a habit, you may need to consider leaving the team before the team leaves you.

Let's now turn our attention to the more formal communication processes of representing the team to others. Table 8.1 lists such strategies.

Table 8.1: Strategies for representing your team

Strategies	Details
1. Identify your audience.	Easier said than done, of course. You may have to rely on the grapevine, contacts, official organisational documents. Is the group sympathetic, hostile, neutral?
2. Match briefs.	Compare what others want you to talk about with what you think you are meant to be doing. Do they match? Have you been given the power to match the responsibility you have been given?

Strategies	Details
3. Identify your message.	What do others want to know? What do they *really* want to know? Is the request for briefing routine or unusual? Check with the grapevine, other teams, insiders. If you've done this before, check your own records and the team's collective memory. Will you tell them what they *want* to hear or what they *need* to hear?
4. Work as a team.	How will you present your team's ideas effectively? If a number of you are to give a presentation, work out a sequence of points to be covered. Vary the content and approach according to the style of the presenter. Strive for variety, but back each other up, and show the interconnectedness of all speakers' points with cross-referencing.
5. Define scope.	What will you tell others? What won't you tell them? How much can you summarise without trivialising? Can you provide them with supplementary written information — e.g., a detailed report they can look at after you've left?
6. Maintain a unified front.	Is there disagreement within the team? Sometimes even consensus cannot mend true differences. Do you wish to reveal these to the outside world? You might express these reservations, or perhaps even give a minority report. Best solution: rank proposals/solutions according to popularity and present to target group. That way, all views are fairly represented, and target group doesn't have to accept your rankings.
7. Check time factors.	Check with the target group's secretary or chairperson to find out how much time you will be given, and whereabouts on the agenda you will appear.
8. Prepare two versions.	Prepare a long and a short version of what you want to say. Be prepared to switch to the short version if pressed, but hold out for the long version if possible. Have a one-page summary which will cover both, for distribution to target-group members. Use point form and schematic graphics where appropriate.
9. Make it visual.	Without trivialising ideas, make them as visual as possible. Use charts, graphs, cause-effect diagrams, flow charts. Poster presentations can be useful, as they are permanent and are usually left on display somewhere — good PR for you. If planning to use audio-visual media, rehearse; hope for the best but expect the worst.
10. Organise material.	How do you wish to organise material? Pick one or a mixture of sequences: chronological/reverse chronological, cause-effect, question-answer, problem-solutions, pros-cons, geographical. Finish up with ranked/prioritised recommendations.
11. Never think or say, 'Isn't it obvious?'	Not necessarily — what may be terribly obvious to the team may be obscure to others. You may be too close to the subject. Do some reality checking by rehearsing in front of an individual or team of same level of technical ignorance/knowledge as target group. You may have blind spots within the team, and should consider bringing in people with different thinking styles.

(continued)

Table 8.1: Strategies for representing your team *(continued)*

Strategies	Details
12. Beware of jargon.	Be careful of using jargon which is acceptable within team, but not necessarily outside it. It only makes other people angry, and if there's too much of it within the team, you may have lost touch with reality anyway.
13. Maintain a 'you' attitude.	What's in it for them? Possibly not the same as what's in it for you. Consider the target group's point of view, biases, and values, more than your own.
14. Strike a balance.	Balance theory with practical considerations, and background with the nitty-gritty. Teams too close to the problem tend to waffle on about theory, background and obscure trivia. Don't be a bore.
15. Rehearse.	Practise in front of the team. Are they happy with what you (and others, if a group presentation) are saying in their name? Have others role-play hostility, objections, obscure questions. Rehearse in the venue if possible. Videotape yourself: observe verbal, non-verbal behaviour: is this the impression you want?
16. Apply the hostile lawyer test.	Apply the 'hostile lawyer test' to everything you say and write, i.e., if you were in a witness box and a hostile lawyer said: 'Do you mean to stand there and tell us that . . .', you would be comfortable in defending your ideas.
17. Do it.	Breathe deeply, have water to drink, move about if it helps stress. You know your stuff.
18. Don't do it now?	If you run out of time, don't be stampeded into an ultra-short performance if you feel it will mutilate your points. Assertively request/offer to come back next time, perhaps leaving written reports for perusal in the interim. This, in fact, might be an advantage.
19. Avoid sidetracking.	Don't get sidetracked — offer to follow up with questioner(s) later. Non-verbally appeal to chair to give you a clear run.
20. Avoid sob stories.	Don't give a barrage of problems, with no solutions. Everyone else does that, and you will stand out if you don't. Similarly, don't try and sneak in special pleading ('If we only had more resources . . .'), or at least not obviously.
21. Remember solidarity forever.	Stay loyal to your team. You should be able to present a range of opinions (see 'A united front') without betraying your own views. Don't be drawn into siding against the team. It isn't nice, and besides, it will get back. Be assertive ('I can't agree, I'm afraid') or stall ('I haven't thought of that. I'll take it back to the team and we'll work on it for you.').
22. Listen.	Apply active listening to remarks of target-group members.
23. Give an action punchline.	What do you want them to do? Suggest clear-cut action steps to target group. Present contingency plans, multiple (perhaps mutually exclusive) recommendations.
24. Pay some courtesies.	Thank the target group for listening, and invite them down to the team's territory to find out more, snoop around, see things from a different perspective.

TEAMS: THE BIG PICTURE

We have covered a lot of ground, gaining insights into how teams do — and don't — work. It is possible to see patterns or stages in team development, and this can help us to determine just what is going on inside a team — particularly if things don't appear to be going all that well.

Teams can be seen to proceed through four stages or phases as summarised in table 9.1.

Table 9.1: Phases of team growth[1]

Phase	What happens
1. Forming	In this stage, team members are attempting to identify just what tasks they should be working on, and also developing a sense of the team's independence.
2. Storming	Here, socio-emotional responses to task demands come to the fore, and conflicts within the group might emerge due to a number of reasons — misunderstanding of role behaviour and norms, conflicting goals, poor feedback and listening, ineffective group decision-making and problem-solving processes.
3. Norming	Here, cohesion begins to develop. Opinions are now stated more readily and are received in a less defensive manner.
4. Performing	Synergy develops via positive role-playing, and the team begins to produce solutions to the problems upon which they are focusing.

It doesn't always work out like this, of course. Sometimes teams self-destruct before reaching stages 3 and 4.

This can often be prevented, however, if team members understand that the phases or stages that all teams and groups go through are developmental stages which are similar to childhood/adolescence/early adulthood/mature adulthood. Thus conflict may not be so much the end of the world as a bit of adolescent trying-on — muscle-flexing and barrier-pushing.

Another model of team development is shown in figure 9.1. What we see here is the sequential and cumulative development of communication skills and processes such as building cohesion via the development of trust, the acceptance and utilisation of individual differences, listening and giving feedback. The entire process begins anew with the finishing off of one task and the taking on of a new one.

The nature of workflow in the traditional bureaucracy comprised — or comprises — an endless belt of routine problems, whereas in many team organisations, workflow is more a matter of only loosely connected projects. While this gives the team organisation considerable flexibility, and gives team members variety and satisfaction, the challenge must be to ensure a flow of projects that stop and start at approximately coordinated points.

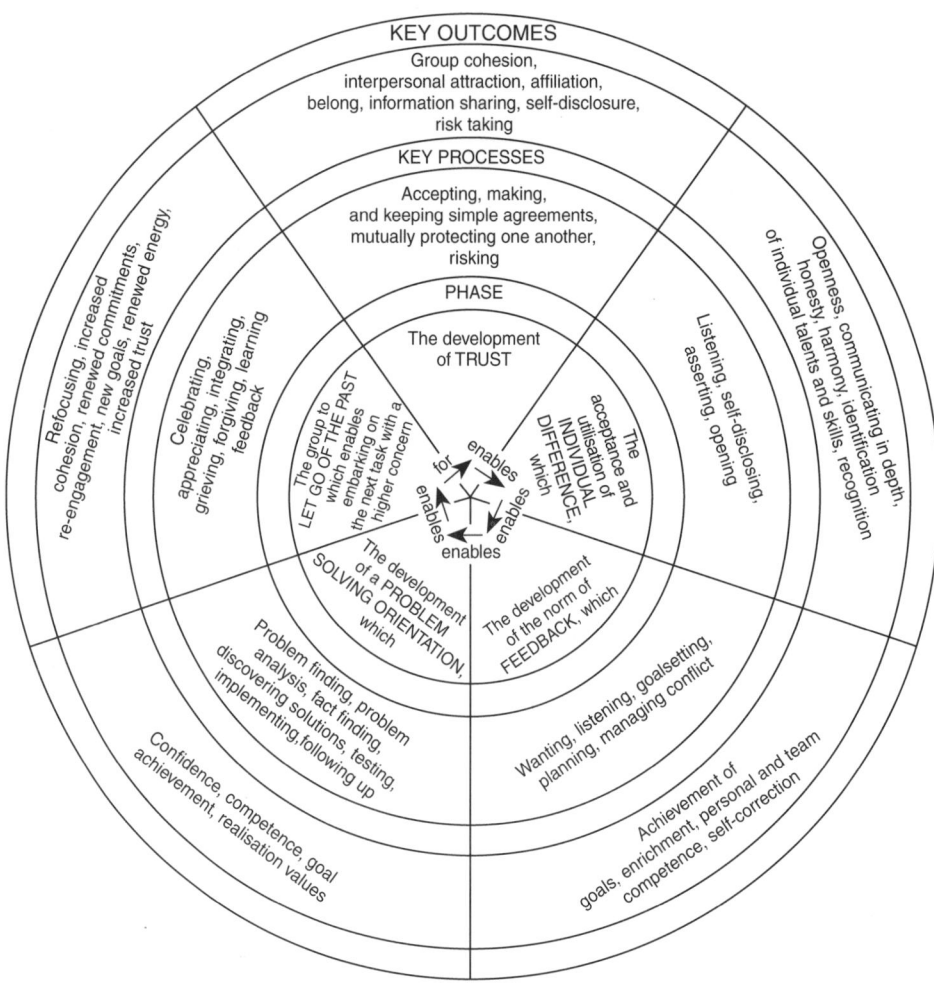

Figure 9.1: An overview of team development

(Source: Mink, Mink and Owen (1987: 42). Reproduced with permission.)

SO ... WHEN SHOULD YOU USE A TEAM?

We have come a long way in analysing communication processes within teams. Along the way, we have looked at the weaknesses, as well as the strengths, of teams. When then should you use a team to perform a particular task? When should you simply do the task yourself? When should you simply delegate it to an individual skilled in that particular task? When should you simply leave it to the routine groups and departments that still comprise the backbone of most organisations? The questionnaire in Exercise H should help you to make these important decisions.

Note

Definitely = D
Possibly = P
Not sure = NS
Unlikely = U
Definitely not = DN

EXERCISE

**H:
TEAMS:
YES OR NO?**

	D	P	NS	U	DN
1. This is a routine problem, soluble by standard operating procedures.					
2. I don't have access — within my personal experience — to a wide enough range of facts to perform the task well.					
3. I have access — within my personal experience — to a wide enough range of opinions and perspectives to perform the task well.					
4. The team has a track record of working with me to ensure that our meetings are effective.					
5. I want the glory and rewards for performing the task all to myself.					
6. I just don't like these people.					
7. The team is skilled in effectively using task- and socio-emotional roles to produce results.					
8. The norms of productivity and tolerance in this team are not good.					
9. The team has excellent listening skills.					
10. Team members' non-verbal communication always seems to contradict their verbal communication.					

(continued)

	D	P	NS	U	DN
11. Team members are unskilled in using various group problem-solving methods (nominal group, consensus, brainstorming, etc.).					
12. Team members are skilled in conflict resolution techniques.					
13. The team has blind spots — too many people think alike.					
14. Sub-tasks need to be done simultaneously.					
15. The task involves substantial problems of coordination of resources, schedules and people.					
16. Team members need to get experience.					
17. If the team fouls up on this operation, the mistake will be forgiven.					
18. Team members are frightened of exercising initiative.					
19. 'I have a control problem, and don't like to delegate. I need to give away a bit of power to the team so that things can get done by others.'					
20. Even if my ideas are wonderful, and I go it alone, will team members feel resentment because they weren't consulted, and undermine the outcome anyway? (If not sure, put yourself in their place.)					

How to score

Use this system of scoring

5	4	3	2	1
D	P	NS	U	DN

for items 2, 4, 7, 9, 12, 14, 15, 16, 17, 19, 20.

Use this system of scoring

1	2	3	4	5
D	P	NS	U	DN

for items 1, 3, 5, 6, 8, 10, 11, 13, 18.

If your score is over 60, consider using a team for the task at hand.
If your score is under 60, consider doing the task yourself.

ENDNOTES
• • • • • • • • • •

CHAPTER 1 — TEAMS

[1] Organisation table — adapted from Dunphy and Dick (1981: 163) and Torres and Spiegel (1990: 4)

[2] Drucker (1992)

[3] Reich (1989b), Nussbaum (1993)

[4] Schilder (1992)

[5] Roberts (1993)

[6] Reich (1983); Peters (1988)

[7] Barry (1991)

[8] Smither (1991)

[9] See Sinclair (1989); Sinclair (1990); Sinclair (1992); Carson (1992); Jaques (1991). Note Jaques' remarks (incorporating a swipe at Drucker's view [Drucker (1988)]about the changing nature of organisations in the future):

'In the long run, therefore, group authority without group accountability is dysfunctional, and group authority with accountability is unacceptable. So images of organisations that are more like symphony orchestras or hospitals or the British raj are surely nothing more than metaphors to express a desired feeling of togetherness — the togetherness produced by a conductor's baton, the shared concern of doctors and nurses for their patients, or the apparent unity of the British civil service in India.'

Jaques argues that individual-based management and hierarchy are inevitable and natural. The key distinction between managers at different levels of the hierarchy of any organisation, he asserts, is the time-frame of the projects or tasks for which managers have responsibility: boundaries occur at time-spans of three months, one year, two years, five years, ten years, and twenty years.

[10] Parker and Slaughter (1988). See also Schilder (1992): 'Although most employees welcome the challenge of making decisions that directly affect them, some feel the stress of added responsibility: "You're asking me to take on more responsibilities, to make decisions I thought you were paid to make", says another Morrisville employee, complaining that he used to be able to go home at the end of his shift without worrying.'

[11] Corporate anorexia — see Kanter (1989). For an analysis of what managers really do, and whether or not they should be downsized into oblivion, see Hilmer (1989).

[12] See Parker and Slaughter (1988: 27)

[13] Sinclair (1989); Sinclair (1990); Sinclair (1992)

[14] Parker and Slaughter (1988)

[15] Collier (1992)

[16] Maddux (1992)

[17] Eunson (1987, chapter 12)

[18] 'Group', 'team' terms Collier (1988)

[19] Analogies or similes are conscious or explicit comparisons of two unlike things to show a poetic insight into similarities, and use the terms 'like' or 'as' — for example, 'She has a heart like stone.' A metaphor is an implicit comparison like an allegory or parable where the words 'like' or 'as' do not appear — for example, 'She has a heart of stone.' Perhaps problems arise with teams and team-building when people slide from analogies into metaphors, and then take metaphors literally.

[20] Note, for example, Keidel (1985), Torres and Spiegel (1990) and Drucker (1993), where comparisons are drawn between different types of work teams in different industries and the different types of teams that occur in sports such as baseball/cricket, football, tennis, volleyball and basketball (such sports differing in terms of whether roles are specialised, whether players can score individually, etc.)

[21] Note Collier's remarks: 'Also, talk about sports teams often conjures up an image which focuses on physical strength and physical aggression. To use this image as being analogous to the business environment may result in an unspoken message that power plays and aggression are appropriate. This message could undermine the participative management style required especially for interdepartmental teams.' Collier (1992)

CHAPTER 2: GROUP DYNAMICS

[1] Hodgetts and Kuratko (1988)

[2] Mitchell et al (1988)

[3] Mitchell et al (1988)

[4] Brightman (1988)

[5] Argyle (1989); Daft (1991)

[6] Newcomb (1950)

[7] Schermerhorn, Hunt and Osburn (1988)

[8] Table adapted from Grasha (1976)

[9] Coch and French (1948)

[10] Kelly (1981); Lee (1980); Littler and Salaman (1984)

[11] Janis and Mann (1977)

[12] Raven and Rubin (1976)

[13] Thomson (1985)

[14] Harvey (1988)

[15] Adapted from Janis and Mann (1977), Kanter (1988), Schermerhorn, Hunt and Osburn (1988), Brilhart and Galanes (1992)

CHAPTER 3: POWER IN TEAMS

[1] Toffler (1990)

[2] See example, Scott and Jaffe (1990)

[3] Note Dumaine:

'Middle managers have always handled two main jobs: supervising people, and gathering, processing and transmitting information. But in growing numbers of companies, self-managed teams are taking over standard supervisory duties such as scheduling work, maintaining quality, even administering pay and vacations. Meanwhile, the ever-expanding power and dwindling cost of computers have transformed information-handling from a difficult, time-consuming job to a far easier and quicker one. Zap! In an instant, historically speaking, the middle manager's traditional functions have vaporised . . .

'What will they, or their late-nineties equivalents, be doing? For an answer, look at those who are now prospering. Call them the new managers, or — better yet — the new non-manager managers. Many, perhaps most, are baby-boomers who bring a radically new set of values to the workplace. The 78 million Americans born between 1946 and 1964 tend to be an irreverent bunch. Many don't see the CEO as much of a hero. In fact, they often think the big guy gets in the way. They like to call themselves leaders, facilitators, sponsors — anything but managers . . . Middle managers who master skills such as team building and entrapreneurship and who acquire broad functional expertise will likely be in the best position to get tomorrow's top corporate jobs. That's because the role of the top executive is becoming more like that of a team player and broker of others' efforts, not that of an autocrat.' Dumaine (1993); see also Geber (1992)

[4] Glaser (1992); Glaser (1991a, 1991b)

[5] Barry (1991: 32): 'Despite the growing popularity of SMTs (Self-Managing Teams), a significant question has gone unanswered: How should leadership be exercised in these leaderless settings — that is, in settings where differences in formal authority either do not exist or are downplayed? The demand for leadership does not simply disappear once the boss is gone. In many ways, actually, the opposite holds true; SMTs require even more leadership than conventional organisational units. In addition to needing task-based leadership (such as project definition, scheduling and resource-gathering), they require leadership around group development processes (developing cohesiveness, establishing effective communication patterns, and so forth). Without the presence of formal authority, power struggles and conflict around both task and process issues surface more often, adding to the overall leadership burden that must be handled by the group. Because many members of SMTs never receive formal training in group process skills, these groups are frequently unstable, tending towards fission rather than fusion.'

[6] See Sinclair (1992); Carson (1992); Smither (1991)

[7] Peters (1988); Sisco (1992)

[8] In 1931, the British Prime Minister, Stanley Baldwin, referred to the press magnates, Lord Beaverbrook and Lord Rothermere, thus: 'What the proprietorship of these papers is aiming at is power, and power without responsibility — the prerogative of the harlot throughout the ages.'

CHAPTER 4: INFORMATION SCANNING: THE BASIS OF COMMUNICATION

[1] Quoted in Ray (1991)

[2] Hanlon and Taylor (1991)

CHAPTER 5: PERCEIVING AND EXPRESSING: COMMUNICATION SKILLS

[1] Stech and Ratliffe (1985)

[2] Argyle (1983)

[3] 'A group that one of us observed had a blind member who could not see the visual regulatory cues. Other members began to be upset at the arrogant and self-centred behaviour they perceived when the blind member seemEd to be talking out of turn or cutting other members short.' (Brilhart and Galanes, 1992: 121)

[4] Brilhart and Galanes (1992: 123, 125)

[5] Drexler (1988)

[6] Brilhart and Galanes (1992: 122, 124)

[7] Woodcock (1989)

[8] Denton (1991)

[9] George (1987)

[10] Facts themselves are less substantial than they might at first appear: it is not uncommon to hear people utter that magnificent tautology, 'true facts'. If a fact is a fact, how can it be untrue? Perhaps the speaker using this phrase betrays his/her uncertainty as to how solid the 'facts' are.

[11] Drucker (1982)

[12] 'The Critic as Artist', *Intention* (1891)

[13] Montgomery (1986)

[14] Bocialietti (1988)

[15] Janis and Mann (1977)

[16] Bocialetti (1988)

[17] Luft (1969)

[18] Poets and writers have been talking about feedback and blind spots long before such terms were invented:

> O wad some Power the giftie gie us
> To see oursels as ithers see us!
> It wad frae monie a blunder free us,
> And foolish notion.
>
> *Robert Burns*

> It is thus with most of us; we are
> what others say we are. We know
> ourselves chiefly by hearsay.
>
> *Eric Hoffer*

I can only know that much of
myself that I have the courage to
confide in you.

John Powell

I am not what I think I am.
I am not what you think I am.
I am what I think you think I am.
Aaron Bleiberg and *Harry Leibling*

[19] See Hargie (1986), Adler and Towne (1990)

[20] Adapted from Hanson (1973)

[21] Adler and Towne (1990)

[22] Reich (1989a)

[23] Adapted from Montgomery (1986), Scholtes et al (1988); see also Ray (1991)

[24] See Eunson (1987, chapter 6)

[25] See example, Berne (1983) for a Transactional Analysis (TA) approach to the psychology of bad communication. You may also find it fruitful to examine a Rational-Emotive Therapy (RET) approach to bad (and stressful) communication — for example, McKay, Davis and Fanning (1981). Both TA and RET approaches are discussed in Eunson (1987) chapters 5 and 7.

[26] Some of the these barriers are adapted from Hargie, Saunders and Dickson (1987); Sigband and Bell (1989); Montgomery (1981); McKay, Davis and Fanning (1983). Other useful approaches to barriers to effective listening are found in Adler and Towne (1990); Adler, Rosenfeld and Towne (1989); and Eunson (1994).

[27] See example, Rogers (1980)

[28] Quoted in Sigband and Bell (1989)

[29] Atwater (1981)

[30] Johnson (1972); Johnson (1991)

CHAPTER 6: DECIDING AND SOLVING: COMMUNICATION SKILLS

[1] See example, Ferris and Wagner (1985)

[2] Moss Kanter (1983: 262): ' "Inequality" and "politics" in team discussions are not generically so bad. After all, the people we are talking about have learned to live with both in the rest of their service in the corporate hierarchy. Dominance of the "best" — most skilled, most informed — participators seems likely to produce better decisions. "Political" discussions may mean that a variety of interests are more accurately reflected in ultimate decisions. So the solution to the problem of lowered commitment that these phenomena create should not lie in expecting the skilled and informed to stay out of discussions or those with special needs or interests to forget them.'

[3] Consensus statement: Schein (1969)

[4] See example, Rees (1991: 140): 'Consensus is not always the best strategy. In some cases, reaching consensus does not result in a better

decision or outcome. Group members are capable of unanimously agreeing on a completely incorrect solution to a problem. On certain occasions, however, consensus remains a highly desirable goal ... Because it takes time and skill, (it) should be reserved for important decisions requiring a high degree of support and commitment from those who will implement the decisions.' Note also Burke (1988: 11): 'Being discriminatory about when and when not to use the team in a group endeavour for consensual decision-making will help ensure time efficiency and a wise use of member energy. Effective teams know when they should meet, and they know how to use their time. I have found the following guidelines useful in deciding when to use the team for consensual decision-making:

- when you do not know who has the most expertise regarding the decision to be made,
- when implementation of the decision will require several people-most, if not all, members of the team,
- when the facts are few — when judgement and opinion are required.

These guidelines are very similar to Vroom and Yetton's more elaborate and detailed decision tree for managers' use in determining how participative to be in decision-making.'

5 Ferris and Wagner (1985)

6 See Thurow (1992)

7 Adapted from Davis (1981: 62), Sinclair (1992: 619): Note Sinclair's perspective: 'The view that "consensus is vital" is also prevalent among management theorists advising on the operation of teams. "Insist on consensus" (they) exhort, paying no attention to the implications of such an imposed "consensus" or to what conflicts and power discrepancies are superficially concealed. Unanimous decisions and easily won "consensus" inevitably betray a condition of group powerlessness rather rather than effectiveness ... the team ideology ... tyrannises because, under the banner of benefits to all, teams are frequently used to camouflage coercion under the pretence of maintaining cohesion; conceal conflict under the guise of consensus; convert conformity into a semblance of creativity; give unilateral decisions a co-determinist seal of approval; delay action in the supposed interests of consultation; legitimise lack of leadership; and disguise expedient arguments and personal agendas.' (Sinclair, 1992: 619, 612)

8 Rawlinson (1981)

9 Quoted in Rawlinson (1981)

10 Way-out ideas: De Bono (1971)

11 Van Gundy (1990); Ferris and Wagner (1985); Burne (1993)

12 Note the view of Linstone (1975: 581–82): 'The specialist is not necessarily the best forecaster. He focuses on a sub-system, and frequently takes no account of the larger system. Reciprocating engine experts in the 1930s forecast that propellor aircraft would be standard up to 1980. Military aircraft experts forecast a succession of manned

bombers beyond the B-52 as primary weapon systems and, for many years, did not consider the replacement of manned bombers by missiles. These experts concentrate on a single logistic curve rather than on the envelope of a series of such curves … A dogmatic drive for conformity, the "tyranny of the majority", sometimes threatens to swamp the single maverick who may actually have better insight than the rest of the "experts" who all agree with each other. This is not unknown in science; it is, in fact, a normal situation in the arduous process of creating new paradigms, i.e., scientific revolutions. In short, a consensus of experts does not assure good judgement or superior estimates.'

[13] Fox (1989)

CHAPTER 7: MEETING AND RESOLVING: COMMUNICATION SKILLS

[1] Adapted from Eunson (1987), Daft (1991), Fletcher (1983), Tropman (1980), Schindler-Rainman (1988)

[2] Fletcher (1983)

[3] Resolving conflict in teams: adapted from Byrt (1980), Luthans (1988)

CHAPTER 9: TEAMS: THE BIG PICTURE

[1] Stages of conflict: Tuckman (1965)

REFERENCE LIST
• • • • • • • • •

Abbott, Jan and Rose, Warren (1991). 'Turning Management Groups into Management Teams', *Journal for Quality and Participation*, December

Adair, John (1987). *Team Building* (London: Pan)

Adler, Ronald B., Rosenfeld, Lawrence B., and Towne, Neil (1989). *Interplay: the Process of Interpersonal Communication* (Fourth Edition) New York: Holt, Rinehart and Winston)

Adler, Ronald B., and Towne, Neil (1990). *Looking Out/Looking In: Interpersonal Communication* (Sixth Edition) (New York: Holt, Rinehart and Winston)

Aldag, Ramon J., and Stearns, Timothy L. (1991). *Management* (Second Edition) (Cincinnati, Ohio: South Western)

Alexander, Mark (1987). 'The Team Effectiveness Critique', in Pfeiffer, J. William (ed.), *The University Associates Instrumentation Kit* (La Jolla, Calif.: University Associates)

Allcorn, Seth (1989). 'Understanding Groups at Work', *Personnel*, August

Argyle, Michael (1989). *The Social Psychology of Work* (New Edition) (Harmondsworth: Penguin)

Atwood, Eastwood (1981). *I Hear You: Listening Skills to Make You a Better Manager* (Englewood Cliffs, New Jersey: Prentice-Hall)

Barry, David (1991). 'Managing the Bossless Team: Lessons in Distributed Leadership', *Organisational Dynamics*, Summer

Belbin, R. Meredith (1981). *Management Teams: Why They Succeed or Fail* (Oxford: Butterworth-Heinemann)

Belbin, Meredith (1993). *Team Roles at Work* (Oxford: Butterworth-Heinemann)

Bennis, Warren G. (1991). 'Retrospective Commentary', in *Participative Management* (Harvard University Press)

Bennis, Warren G. and Slater, Philip (1991). 'Democracy is Inevitable', in *Participative Management* (Harvard University Press). (Originally in *Harvard Business Review*, March/April, 1964)

Berne, Eric (1983). *Games People Play: The Psychology of Interpersonal Relationships* (Harmondsworth: Penguin)

Blanchard, Kenneth, Carew, Donald, Parisi-Carew, Eunice (1990). *The One-Minute Manager Builds High-Performing Teams* (New York: William Morrow)

Bocialetti, Gene (1988). 'Teams and the Managment of Emotion', in Reddy/Jamison (eds.)

Bone, Diane (1988). *The Business of Listening: A Practical Guide to Effective Listening* (Palo Alto, Calif.: Crisp Publications)

Boyett, Joseph H., and Conn, Henry P. (1991). *Workplace 2000: The Revolution Reshaping American Business* (New York: Dutton)

Bostrom, Robert P., Watson, Richard T., and Kinney, Susan T. (1992). *Computer-Augmented Teamwork: A Guided Tour* (Florence, Kentucky: Van Nostrand Reinhold)

Brightman, H. J. (1988). *Group Problem-Solving: An Improved Managerial Approach* (Georgia University: College of Business Administration Press)

Brilhart, John K. and Galanes, Gloria J. (1992). *Effective Group Discussion* (Seventh Ed.) (Dubuque, Iowa: Wm. C. Brown)

Bucholz, Steve, and Roth, Thomas (ed. Hess, Karen) (1987). *Creating the High Performance Team* (New York: Wiley)

Bureau of Business Practice (1992). *Team Building for Managers, Supervisors and Team Leaders* (Englewood Cliffs, New Jersey: Bureau of Business Practice/Prentice-Hall)

Burke, W. Warner (1988). 'Team Building', in Reddy/Jamison (eds.)

Burley-Allen, Madlyn (1982). *Listening: The Forgotten Skill* (New York: Wiley)

Burne, Jerome (1993). 'Brainstorming Debunked', The *Australian*, January 20

Byrt, J. William (1980). *The Human Variable: Text and Cases in Organisational Behaviour* (Sydney: McGraw-Hill)

Capps, Randall (1981). *Communication for the Business and Professional Speaker* (New York: Macmillan)

Carlisle, Arthur Elliott (1988). 'An Abilene Defence: Commentary 2', *Organisational Dynamics*, Summer

Carr, Clay (1991). 'Managing Self-Managing Workers', *Training and Development*, September

Carr, Clay (1992). *Teampower: Lessons from America's Top Companies on Putting Teampower to Work* (Englewood Cliffs, New Jersey: Prentice-Hall)

Carson, Neil (1992). 'The Trouble with Teams', *Training*, August

Coch, L. and French, J. (1948). 'Overcoming Resistance to Change', *Human Relations*, Vol. 2(4)

Colantuono, Susan L., and Schnidman, Ava A. (1988). 'E Pluribus Unum: Building Multifunctional Work Teams', in Reddy/Jamison (eds.)

Collier, Marilyn R. (1992). 'Team Building May Not Be Appropriate for Groups', *OD Practitioner*, June

Craig-Cooper, Sir Michael, and De Backer, Phillipe (1993). *The Management Audit: How to Create an Effective Management Team* (London: Pitman/Financial Times)

Daft, Richard L. (1991). *Management* (Second Edition) (Fort Worth, Texas: Dryden Press)

Davis, Keith (1981). *Human Behaviour at Work: Organisational Behaviour* (New York: McGraw-Hill)

De Bono, Edward (1971). *Lateral Thinking for Management* (London: McGraw-Hill)

Delbecq, Andre L., Van de Ven, Andrew H., and Gustafson, David H. (1975). *Group Techniques for Program Planning: A Guide to Nominal Group and Delphi Processes* (Glenview, Ill.: Scott, Foresman)

Denton, D. Keith (1991). *Horizontal Management: Beyond Total Customer Satisfaction* (New York: Lexington Books)

Douglas, Merrill E., and Douglas, Donna N. (1992). *Time Management for Teams* (New York: Amacom)

Drexler, Allen B., Sibbet, David, and Forrester, Russell H. (1988). 'The Team Performance Model', in Reddy/Jamison (eds.)

Drucker, Peter F. (1982). *The Effective Executive* (London: Pan)

Drucker, Peter F. (1988). 'The Coming of the New Organisation', *Harvard Business Review*, January–February

Drucker, Peter F. (1992). 'The New Society of Organisations', *Harvard Business Review*, September-October

Drucker, Peter F. (1993). *Post-Capitalist Society* (Oxford: Butterworth-Heinemann)

Dumaine, Brian (1993) 'The New Non-Manager Managers', *Fortune*, 22 February

Dunphy, Dexter, and Dick, Robert (1981). *Organisational Change by Choice* (Sydney: McGraw-Hill)

Eitington, Julius E. (1989). *The Winning Trainer* (Houston, Texas: Gulf Publishing)

English, Linda (1988). 'The Tyranny of Teamness', *Australian Accountant*, November

Eunson, Baden (1987). *Behaving: Managing Yourself and Others* (Sydney: McGraw-Hill)

Eunson, Baden (1990). 'Group Dynamics', in McWalters, M. (ed.) *Understanding Psychology* (Sydney: McGraw-Hill)

Eunson, Baden (1994). *Negotiation Skills* (Milton, Queensland: Jacaranda-Wiley)

Ferris, Gerald R., and Wagner, John A. (1985). 'Quality Circles in the United States: A Conceptual Re-evaluation', *The Journal of Applied Behavioural Science*, Vol. 21, No. 2

Fletcher, Douglas S. (1991). *Management Control in Today's Teamwork Organisation: How to Get Things Done Without Exercising Direct Authority* (King of Prussia, PA: Organisation Design and Development)

Fletcher, Winston (1983). *Meetings, Meetings: How to Manipulate Them and Have More Fun* (London: Michael Joseph)

Fox, William M. (1989). 'The Improved Nominal Group Technique (INGT)', *Journal of Management Development*, Vol. 18, No. 1

Fulop, Liz, with Frith, Faye and Hayward, Harold (1992). *Management for Australian Business: A Critical Text* (South Melbourne: Macmillan)

Gadon, Herman (1988). 'The Newcomer and the Ongoing Work Group', in Reddy/Jamison (eds.)

Gaegler, Margaret (1989). 'Overcoming Groupthink', *Journal for Quality and Participation*, June

Galanes, Gloria J., and Brilhart, John K. (1991). *Communicating in Groups: Applications and Skills* (Dubuque, Iowa: Wm. C. Brown)

Galagan, Patricia A. (1992). 'Beyond Hierarchy: The Search for High Performance', *Training and Development*, August

Geber, Beverly (1992). 'From Manager into Coach', *Training*, February

George, Paul S. (1987). 'Team Building', *Personnel Journal*, November

Glaser, Rollin (1991a). *How Independent is Our Team? The Gulowsen Autonomy Scales* (King of Prussia, PA: Organisation Design and Development)

Glaser, Rollin (1991b). *Learning to be a Self-Managing Team* (King of Prussia, PA: Organisation Design and Development)

Glaser, Rollin (1992). *Moving Your Team Toward Self-Management* (King of Prussia, PA: Organisation Design and Development)

Goodall, H. Lloyd. Sr. (1990). *Small Group Communication in Organisations* (Dubuque, Iowa: Wm. C. Brown)

Goodman, Paul S. and Associates (1986). *Designing Effective Work Groups* (San Francisco: Jossey-Bass)

Gordon, Jack (1992). 'Work Teams: How Far Have They Come?', *Training*, October

Grasha, Anthony (1976). *Practical Applications of Psychology* (Englewood Cliffs, New Jersey: Prentice-Hall)

Hackman, J. Richard (ed.) (1991). *Groups That Work (And Those That Don't): Creating Conditions for Effective Teamwork* (San Francisco: Jossey-Bass)

Handy, Charles (1990). *Inside Organisations* (London: BBC Books)

Hanlon, Susan C., and Taylor, Robert R. (1991). 'An Examination of Changes in Work Group Communication Behaviours Following Institution of a Gainsharing Plan', *Group & Organisation Studies*, Vol. 16, No. 3

Hanson, Phillip C. (1973). 'The Johari Window: A Model for Soliciting and Giving Feedback', in Pfeiffer, J. William and Jones, John E. (eds.) *The 1973 Annual Handbook for Group Facilitators* (San Diego, California: University Associates, Inc.)

Hargie, Owen, 'The Skill of Self-Disclosure', in Hargie (1989)

Hargie, Owen (ed.) (1989). *A Handbook of Communication Skills* (London: Routledge)

Hargie, Owen, Saunders, Christine, and Dickson, David (1987). *Social Skills in Interpersonal Communication* (Second Edition) (London: Croom Helm)

Harper, Bob, and Harper, Ann (1992). *Succeeding as a Self-Directed Work Team: 20 Important Questions Answered* (Mohegan Lake, NY: MW Corporation)

Harvey, Jerry B. (1988). 'The Abilene Paradox: The Management of Agreement' (With 'Abilene Revisited: An Epilogue'), *Organisational Dynamics*, Summer

Hastings, Colin, Bixby, Peter, and Chaudhry-Lawton, Rani (1986). *The Superteam Solution: Successful Teamworking in Organisations* (Aldershot, Hants.: Gower)

Hathaway, Patti (1990). *Giving and Receiving Criticism: Your Key to Interpersonal Success* (Los Altos, California: Crisp Publications)

Heaney, Donald (1989). *Cut-throat Teammates: Achieving Effective Teamwork Among Professionals* (Homewood, Ill.: Business One Irwin)

Hicks, Robert F., and Bone, Diane (1990). *Self-Managing Teams: Creating and Managing Self-Managed Work Groups* (Los Altos, California: Crisp Publications)

Hilmer, Frederick G. (1989). 'Real Jobs for Real Managers', *The McKinsey Quarterly*, Summer, 1989

Hirschhorn, Larry (1991). *Managing in the New Team Environment: Skills, Tools and Methods* (Reading, Mass.: Addison-Wesley)

Hodgetts, R. M. (1980). *Modern Human Relations* (Hinsdale, Illinois: Dryden Press)

Hodgetts, R. M. and Kuratko, D. L. (1988). *Management* (Second Edition) (New York: Harcourt, Brace Jovanovich)

Hogan, R. Craig and Champagne, David W. (1980). 'Personal Style Inventory', in Pfeiffer, J. William, and Jones, John E. (eds.), *The Annual Handbook for Group Facilitators* (La Jolla, California: University Associates)

Hughes, Bob (1991). '25 Stepping Stones for Self-Directed Work Teams', *Training*, December

Hunt, John (1979). *Managing People at Work* (London: McGraw-Hill)

Jacobs, R. C., and Everett, J. G. (1988). 'The Importance of Team Building in a High-Tech Environment', *JEIT*, Vol. 12, No. 4

Janis, Irving, and Mann, Leon (1977). *Decision-Making: A Psychological Analysis of Conflict, Choice and Commitment* (New York: Free Press)

Jaques, Elliott (1991). 'In Praise of Hierarchy', in *Participative Management* (Harvard, Massachusetts: Harvard University Press)

Johnson, David W. and Johnson, Frank P. (1991). *Joining Together: Group Theory and Group Skills* (Fourth Edition) (Needham Heights, MA: Prentice-Hall)

Johnson, H. Thomas (1992). *Relevance Regained: From Top-Down Control to Bottom-Up Empowerment* (New York: Free Press)

Kanter, Rosabeth Moss (1983). *The Change Masters: Innovation for Productivity in the American Corporation* (New York: Simon and Schuster)

Kanter, Rosabeth Moss (1988). 'An Abilene Defence: Commentary 1', *Organisational Dynamics*, Summer, 1988

Kanter, Rosabeth Moss (1989). *When Giants Learn to Dance: Mastering the Challenges of Strategies, Management and Careers in the 1990s* (New York: Simon and Schuster)

Katz, Sally N. (1991). 'Power Skills for Effective Meetings', *Training and Development*, July

Katzenbach, Jon R. and Smith, Douglas K. (1993). *The Wisdom of Teams: Creating the High-Performance Organisation* (Boston, Mass.: Harvard Business School Press)

Keidel, Robert (1985). *Game Plans* (New York: E. P. Dutton)

Kelly, John E. (1981). *Scientific Management, Job Redesign and Work Performance* (New York: Academic Press)

Kindler, Herbert S. (1988). *Managing Disagreement Constructively: Conflict Management in Organisations* (Los Altos, California: Crisp Publications)

Kinlaw, Dennis C. (1991). *Developing Superior Work Teams: Building Quality and the Competitive Edge* (Lexington, Massachusetts/San Diego, California: Lexington Books/University Associates, Inc.)

Koontz, Harold, O'Donnell, Cyril, and Weihrish, Heinz (1980). *Management* (Seventh Edition) (New York: McGraw-Hill)

Kormenski, Chuck, and Mozenter, Andrew (1987). 'A New Model of Team Building: A Technology for Today and Tomorrow', in Pfeiffer, J. William (ed.) *The 1987 Annual Handbook for Group Facilitators* (La Jolla, California: University Associates)

Larson, Carl E. and LaFasto, Frank M. J. (1989). *Teamwork: What Must Go Right/What Can Go Wrong* (Newbury Park, California: Sage)

Lawler, Edward E. (1988). 'Substitutes for Hierarchy', *Organisational Dynamics*, Summer

Lee, James A. (1980). *The Gold and the Garbage in Management Theories and Prescriptions* (Athens, Ohio: Ohio University Press)

Leigh, Andrew and Maynard, Michael (1993). *Ace Teams: Creating Star Performance in Business* (Oxford: Butterworth-Heinemann)

Lefton, Robert E. (1988). 'Communication: The Eight Barriers to Teamwork', *Personnel Journal*, January

Linstone, Harold A. (1975). 'Eight Basic Pitfalls: A Checklist', in Linstone, Harold A. and Turoff, Murray (eds.), *The Delphi Method: Techniques and Applications* (Reading, Mass: Addison-Wesley)

Littler, C. R. and Salaman, G. (1984). *Class at Work: The Design, Allocation and Control of Jobs* (London: Batsford)

Luft, Joseph (1969). *Of Human Interaction* (Palo Alto, California: Natural Press)

Mackay, Matthew, Davis, Martha, and Fanning, Patrick (1981). *Thoughts and Feelings: The Art of Cognitive Stress Intervention* (Oakland, California: New Harbinger Press)

Mackay, Matthew, Davis, Martha, and Fanning, Patrick (1983). *Messages: The Communication Skills Book* (Oakland, California: New Harbinger Press)

McPhee, Joan, and McNicol, Bruce (1992). 'New Direction for Supervisor Training', *Training Australia*, March

Maddux, Robert B. (1992). *Team Building: An Exercise in Leadership* (Revised Edition) (Los Altos, California: Crisp Publications)

Marchington, Mick (1992). *Managing the Team: A Guide to Successful Employee Involvement* (Oxford: Blackwell)

Margerison, Charles and McCann, Dick (1991). *Team Management: Understanding How People Work Together* (Melbourne: Information Australia)

Mink, Oscar G., Mink, Barbara P., and Owen, Keith Q. (1987). *Groups at Work* (Englewood Cliffs, New Jersey: Education Technology Publications)

Mitchell, Terence R., Dowling, Peter J., Kabanoff, Boris V., and Larson, James R. (1988). *People in Organisations: An Introduction to Organisational Behaviour in Australia* (Sydney: McGraw-Hill)

Montgomery, Bob (1986). *Working Together: A Practical Guide to Collaborative Decision-Making* (Melbourne: Nelson)

Montgomery, Robert L. (1981). *Listening Made Easy* (New York: Amacom)

Neuhaser, Peg C. (1990). *Tribal Warfare in Organisations* (New York: Harper and Row)

Newcomb, T. M. (1950). *Social Psychology* (New York: Dryden)

Nussbaum, Bruce (1993). 'Hot Products: Smart Design is the Common Thread', *Business Week*, June 7

Orsburn, Jack D., Moran, Linda, Musselwhite, Ed and Zenger, John H. (1990). *Self-Directed Work Teams: The New American Challenge* (Homewood, Illinois: Business One Irwin)

Parker, Glenn M. (1991). *Team Players and Teamwork: The New Competitive Business Strategy* (San Francisco: Jossey-Bass)

Parker, Mike, and Slaughter, Jane (1988). *Choosing Sides: Unions and the Team Concept* (Boston: South End Press)

Peters, Tom (1988). *Thriving on Chaos: Handbook for a Management Revolution* (London: Macmillan)

Petrock, Frank (1991). 'Ford's Teamwork Training Gets Employees Involved', *Human Resources Professional*, Vol. 3, No. 3 (Spring)

Phillips, Nicola (1992). *Managing International Teams* (London: Financial Times/Pitman)

Randolph, W. Alan and Posner, Barry Z. (1992). *Getting the Job Done! Managing Project Teams and Task Forces for Success* (Englewood Cliffs, New Jersey: Prentice-Hall)

Raven, B. and Rubin, J. (1976). *Social Psychology: People in Groups* (New York: John Wiley)

Rawlinson, J. Geoffrey (1981). *Creative Thinking and Brainstorming* (Wetmead, Farnborough Hants: Gower)

Ray, Darrel W. (1991). 'Overcoming Conflict with Structured Feedback', *Journal for Quality and Participation*, December

Reddy, W. Brendan, and Jamison, Kaleel (eds) (1988). *Team Building: Blueprints for Productivity and Satisfaction* (Alexandria, Virginia/ San Diego, California: NTL Institute for Applied Behavioural Science/ University Associates, Inc.)

Rees, Fran (1991). *How to Lead Work Teams: Facilitation Skills* (San Diego, California: Pfeiffer)

Reich, Robert B. (1983). *The Next American Frontier* (New York: Times Books)

Reich, Robert B. (1989a). *The Resurgent Liberal: and Other Unfashionable Prophecies* (New York: Times Books)

Reich, Robert B. (1989b). 'The Quiet Path to Technological Pre-eminence', *Scientific American* (October)

Reich, Robert B. (1991). 'Entrepreneurship Reconsidered: The Team as Hero', in *Participative Management* (Harvard, Massachusetts: Harvard University Press)

Roberts, Peter (1993). 'Teamwork Serves Up an Ace for Manufacturers', The *Australian Financial Review*, August 16, p. 2

Rogers, Carl (1980). *A Way of Being* (Houghton Mifflin: Boston)

Rose, Michael (1988). *Industrial Behaviour* (Second Edition) (Harmondsworth: Penguin)

Saul, Peter (1991). *Strategic Team Leadership: Creating Winning Teams for the 1990s* (Sydney: McGraw-Hill)

Schein, Edgar (1969). *Process Consultation* (Reading, Mass: Addison-Wesley)

Schermerhorn, John R. Jr, Hunt, James G., and Osborn, Richard N. (1988). *Managing Organisational Behaviour* (Third Edition) (New York: John Wiley & Sons)

Schilder, Jana (1992). 'Work Teams Boost Productivity', *Personnel Journal*, February

Schindler-Rainman, Eva (1988). 'Team Building in Voluntary Organisations', in Reddy and Jamison

Scholtes, Peter R. (and other contributors) (1988). *The Team Handbook: How to Use Teams to Improve Quality* (Madison, Wisconsin: Joiner Associates, Inc.)

Schuster, Jay R. and Zingheim, Patricia K. (1992). *The New Pay: Linking Employee and Organisational Performance* (New York: Lexington Books)

Scott, Cynthia D., and Jaffe, Dennis T. (1991). *Empowerment: A Practical Guide for Success* (Los Altos, California: Crisp Publications)

Shonk, James H. (1992). *Team-Based Organisations* (Homewood, Illinois: Irwin)

Sigband, Norman B., and Bell, Arthur H. (1989). *Communication for Management and Business* (Fifth Edition) (Glenview, Illinois: Scott, Foresman)

Sinclair, Amanda (1989). *The Tyranny of the Team* (Parkville, Melbourne: University of Melbourne Graduate School of Management)

Sinclair, Amanda (1990). 'Myths About Teamwork', The *Weekend Australian*, April 7–8, 1990

Sinclair, Amanda (1992). 'The Tyranny of a Team Ideology', *Organisation Studies*, Vol. 13, No. 4

Sisco, Rebecca (1992). 'Put Your Money Where Your Teams Are', *Training*, July

Smith, Bernard Babington, and Sharp, Alan (1986). *Manager and Team Development: Ideas and Principles Underlying Coverdale Training* (Oxford: Heinemann Professional)

Smither, Robert D. (1991). 'The Return of the Authoritarian Manager', *Training*, November

Spencer, John, and Pruss, Adrian (1992). *Managing Your Team: How to Organise People for Maximum Results* (London: Piatkus)

Stech, Ernest, and Ratliffe, Sharon A. (1985). *Effective Group Communication: How to Get Action by Working in Groups* (Lincolnwood, Illinois: National Textbook Company)

Stoner, James A., Collins, Roger R., and Yetton, Phillip W. (1985). *Management in Australia* (Sydney: Prentice-Hall)

Teasedale, T. C. (1976). *Social Psychology: A Two-Year Course* (Windsor, Victoria: Lloyd O'Neill)

Thiagarajan, Sivasailem (1991). 'Take Five for Better Brainstorming', *Training and Development Journal*, February

Thomson, J. G. (1985). *Psychological Aspects of Nuclear War* (Chichester, West Sussex: British Psychological Society/John Wiley and Sons)

Thurow, Lester (1992). *Head to Head: The Coming Economic Battle Among Japan, Europe and America* (New York: Morrow)

Tjosvold, Dean (1991). *Team Organisation: An Enduring Competitive Advantage* (Chichester, West Sussex: John Wiley and Sons)

Tjosvold, Dean W., and Tjosvold, Mary (1991). *Leading the Team Organisation: How to Create an Enduring Competitive Advantage* (New York: Lexington Books/Macmillan, Inc.)

Toffler, Alvin (1990). *Powershift: Knowledge, Wealth and Violence at the Edge of the 21st Century* (New York: Bantam)

Torres, Cresencio, and Spiegel, Jerry (1990). *Self-Directed Work Teams: A Primer* (San Diego, California: Pfeiffer and Co.)

Tropman, John E. (1980). *Effective Meetings: Improving Group Decision-Making* (Beverly Hills: Sage)

Tuckman, Bruce W. (1965). 'Developmental Sequence in Small Groups', *Psychological Bulletin*, 63: 384–99

Tyson, Trevor (1989). *Working with Groups* (South Melbourne: Macmillan)

Van Gundy, Arthur B. (1990). *Techniques of Structured Problem-Solving* (Second Edition) (New York: Van Nostrand Reinhold)

Varney, Glen H. (1990). *Building Productive Teams: An Action Guide and Source Book* (San Francisco: Jossey-Bass)

Wellins, Richard S., Byham, William C., and Wilson, Jeanne M. (1991). *Empowered Teams: Creating Self-Directed Work Groups that Improve Quality, Productivity and Participation* (San Francisco: Jossey-Bass)

Wolvin, Andrew, and Coakley, Carolyn Gwynn (1992). *Listening* (Fourth Edition) (Dubuque, Iowa: Wm. C. Brown)

Woodcock, Mike (1989). *Team Development Manual* (Second Edition) (Aldershot, Hants.: Gower)

Zenger, John H., Musselwhite, Ed, Hurson, Kathleen and Perrin, Craig (1994). *Leading Teams: Mastering the New Role* (Homewood, Ill.: Business One Irwin)

INDEX

• • • • • • • • •